kamera
BOOKS

www.kamerabooks.com

Douglas Keesey

CONTEMPORARY EROTIC CINEMA

kamera
BOOKS

First published in 2012 by Kamera Books
an imprint of Oldcastle Books,
PO Box 394, Harpenden, Herts, AL5 1XJ
www.kamerabooks.com

ISBN
978-1-84243-363-8
978-1-84243-645-5 (kindle)
978-1-84243-646-2 (epub)
978-1-84243-647-9 (pdf)

Typeset by Elsa Mathern
Printed and bound CPI Group (UK) Ltd, Croydon, CR0 4YY

For Helen,
my one true love

CONTENTS

INTRODUCTION

Sex is sex, right? You know it when you see it, and you certainly know what it means. A sex scene needs no interpretation; its sense is self-evident. It is what it is.

Well, picture a couple having sex. Are they 'fucking' or 'making love', and how can you tell the difference? Could it be both? If the man is on top of the woman, is he in a position of dominance or does it have nothing to do with gender hierarchy? If we call this the 'missionary position', does that give it religious sanction or remind us of patriarchal religion's history of subjugating women?

Next we see the two engaged in anal intercourse, with him 'taking her from behind'. Describing it this way might make it sound disturbingly forceful and animalistic, but this could be exactly what she told him she wants to play at doing. If she then puts on a strap-on dildo and 'pegs' him, are they opening up new avenues for pleasure, or does resorting to a sex toy mean that their relationship is so tired it now needs artificial aids?

Let's say he 'goes down on her'. 'Giving her head' could be a special favour, bowing down before the female sex in a way that some men won't do, or it might be *his* preference and something she reluctantly (or readily) gives to him. If he now stands above her while receiving oral sex, is he empowered as the penetrator or is she the one who has him at her mercy, holding his vulnerable member in her mouth? If they lie side by side and engage in 69ing, does this make them equals?

Does it matter if the couple having sex are virginal or experienced, married or adulterous, in their bedroom or at a motel? What if they're of different ages or races, or both of the same sex? What if there are three or more of them in bed together – or only one self-pleasuring and being watched by someone else?

The fact is that, in any given scene, what 'sex' means will change depending on the particular way it is represented and the particular words we use to describe it. As Linda Williams points out, sex 'is not a stable truth that cameras and microphones either "catch" or don't catch. It is a constructed, mediated, performed act',[1] conveyed to us by the medium of film which includes, omits, emphasises and editorialises with every angle, cut, actor's gesture and word of dialogue.

This book looks at the representation of sex in films over the last 40 years,[2] studying erotic scenes by directors around the world.[3] Contemporary erotic cinema begins with the sexual revolution in the late 1960s. The relaxation of religious restrictions and legal bans on various kinds of sexual behaviour, combined with the widespread availability of birth control, led to a more liberal sexual climate. Feminist, gay, lesbian, transgender and queer groups moved society towards an acceptance of a wider range of sexual identities, acts and affects. Rather than heterosexual monogamy as the presumed and enforced norm (females were expected to act 'feminine' and to pair-bond for life with a man, having sex for the purpose of procreation), other possibilities for sexual satisfaction became available. Reflecting or promoting these changes in sexual mores, films began to show a much broader spectrum of intimate acts, including many formerly taboo behaviours. In the US, what was essentially a system of censorship, the Motion Picture Production Code, was replaced in 1968 by a ratings system that theoretically allowed directors to include whatever they wanted in their films. These would then be classified based on content as a service for the viewing public, who were thereby informed of what was in the films and free to see whichever ones they chose.

Thus, one tendency in contemporary erotic cinema is towards increasing liberalisation. Some of the restraints of civilisation are lifted, and characters are freed to pursue pleasure in ways *they* find to be instinctually gratifying. *American Pie* reduces the shame of masturbation, making it hilarious – and homey as apple pie. Japan's *The Snake of June* also works through shame – this time regarding female pleasure – and finds that exhibitionism is one way to overcome it. Religious repression of women's sexuality is lasciviously lifted in Italy's *Behind Convent Walls*, and a boy's healthy sexual awakening occurs despite fears of damnation in Australia's *The Devil's Playground*. *Y Tu Mamá También* takes two Mexican boys on a journey from macho defensiveness to homoeroticism, while *Brokeback Mountain* shows America that cowboys – the very archetypes of masculinity – can also be gay. England's *The Attendant* brings a black museum guard and a white visitor together in a sado-masochistic relationship that plays with racist domination as a way of moving past it, while *The Lover* presents a passionate liaison between a French girl and a Chinese man, challenging taboos on interracial and cross-generational sex. *Me and You and Everyone We Know* dares to represent childhood sexuality as natural, healthy and frequently humorous in its awkward stages of development. In *Black Swan*, masturbation and lesbian oral sex are validated as moments of sexual self-discovery for a young woman. The man in *Transamerica* is supported in his belief that to find himself he must become a woman, and the intersex character in *XXY* is encouraged in her hope that she need not mutilate herself to become male or female, but can instead remain whole as both.

Male or female, masculine or feminine, heterosexual or homosexual – these either/or choices have increasingly become both/and possibilities. The limited option of married or single has been expanded to include premarital, extramarital or non-marital sex with more than one partner, serially or simultaneously. *Ken Park* ends with a threesome and *Shortbus* climaxes in an orgy, and these are represented as utopian alternatives to the sexual repression, jealousy and possessiveness typical of compulsory monogamy. Similarly, restrictions on what is and is not an erogenous zone have been opened up beyond the merely genital (the penetrative vaginal intercourse of conservative morality) to include oral, anal and potentially all other parts of the body. Fellatio figures largely in *Now & Later*; cunnilingus is central to *In the Cut*; and *I Love You, I Don't* is all about anal intimacy. In *Beautiful Thing*, a boy's back is eroticised, and in *9½ Weeks* it is a woman's belly button. Feet are tantalisingly tickled in *Mirch*; body hair is stroked in *Fur*; and the entire epidermis is excited in *The Man Who Fell to Earth*. In contemporary erotic cinema, the body is increasingly deterritorialised, with its sexuality becoming more and more polymorphously perverse.

Moviemakers' attempts over the last four decades to expand the boundaries of sex on film have led to some battles with the ratings boards, which have tended to push back in the name of conservative social norms. While apparently applied only after the fact as an advisory notice regarding film content, the NC-17 rating has operated as a form of *de facto* censorship in the US. Because some movie studios won't finance NC-17 films – and some media outlets won't advertise them and some theatre chains won't show them – the pressure is on directors to cut their films in order to receive an R rating or to censor themselves during filmmaking, not even allowing their imaginations to go into sexually adventurous 'NC-17' territory. Despite its not being erect, shots of Ewan McGregor's male member were cut from *Young Adam* for an R rating, prompting the actor to remark, 'If I'd blown away 5,000 people with a semi-automatic machine gun, that would be fine. But I showed my penis.'[4] Peter Sarsgaard, an actor who has not shied away from full-frontal nudity (*Kinsey*, *The Centre of the World*), has noted that 'The ratings board can only handle so much penis. They can handle a lot of tits and ass. If you have a penis in a movie, you get a certain amount of time with that penis before you become NC-17.'[5]

And, if 'tits and ass' are allowed, erotic exposure of the female sex is not, as William H Macy and Maria Bello found out about their film *The Cooler*. To avoid an NC-17, a 1½-second shot of his mouth moving up from her mons after cunnilingus had to be cut. 'Apparently, you cannot show pubic hair in a sexual situation', commented Bello after her meeting with the ratings board.[6] This same board also took issue with another scene of female-centred pleasure in the movie *Coming Soon*, where a young woman reaches climax from a jacuzzi water-jet. This scene was deemed 'too lurid' for an R rating,[7] even though there were no shots of her below the waist and the only 'private part' on display was her ecstatic face. Director Colette Burson has called attention to the gender bias of these rating practices: 'Almost any time a girl orgasmed, the board wanted me to cut the scene by 75 per cent, even though she was 18. I was told specifically that the board has a problem with young girls' orgasms. I got on the phone with a woman from the board and said I can't help but point out that, if it were boys, you wouldn't have a problem. She said that may well be true; however, it is the job of the board to judge for parents across America and, if the parents were to see the movie, they would be judging it with a double standard and therefore the board must judge it that way, too.'[8] Director Allison Anders sums up the situation with movie ratings by arguing that they attempt to exert an overall sexual repression: 'There's a denial of female pleasure or a denial of pleasure, period – male pleasure, too; you can barely see anything of a male body on the screen. I think that nobody gets to come, basically. I think that that's what it is.'[9]

Certainly, one thing you're not likely to see in a 'legitimate' mainstream theatre is a 'cum shot'. In the UK, the BBFC insisted on cutting an ejaculation shot from *The Pornographer*, even though this was an art-house film *about* porn and not porn *per se*, in order to grant it an 18 certificate. Viewers had to seek out a licensed sex shop if they wanted to see this scene's dramatic climax. The BBFC deleted a close-up penetration shot from *Baise-moi* because it occurred during a rape scene and could be viewed as eroticising violence, despite the fact that it could also be seen as condemning the rapists and the porn-fuelled culture which helped to create them. Before granting the film an R, the US ratings board wanted a scene excised from *Storytelling* in which a black man roughly sodomises a white woman while having her repeat, 'Fuck me, nigger.' Though his thrusting buttocks were the ostensible reason for the cut, the sexualised violence, particularly in an interracial context, may have contributed to the discomfort of the board, which was ready to force its notion of proper sexual conduct and race relations on all viewers. Rather than delete the scene, director Todd Solondz highlighted the board's repression by blocking out the offending buttocks with a box: '*Storytelling* is the only studio movie where the censorship is perfectly clear, the only studio movie with a big red box covering up a shot. I take pride in that,' Solondz has said.[10]

Yet, despite these high-profile cases of actual or *de facto* censorship, more liberal attitudes to sex have led even the ratings boards to loosen their restrictions. A number of films that would formerly have been subjected to substantial cuts or slapped with an NC-17 have been approved for an R rating and released to mainstream American audiences. Some of these movies may have 'slipped past the censor' by presenting sex within the reassuring context of a familiar genre, such as melodrama (*Unfaithful*'s energetic coupling), comedy (*Scary Movie*'s geyser-like ejaculation) or noir (*8mm*'s snuff porn). However, other R-rated films – with no generic 'alibi' – are more clearly the sign of greater social acceptance of sexual freedom: sado-masochism (*Secretary*), male nudity (*Boogie Nights*), bisexuality (*Kinsey*), homosexuality (*Brokeback Mountain*) and lesbianism (*Black Swan*). In the UK, *Intimacy* (with unsimulated fellatio) and *9 Songs* (with actual penetration) were both passed uncut with 18-certificates for theatrical release, as was *Shame* which, in focusing on a sex addict, has pervasive sexual images including voyeurism, nudity, rear-entry intercourse, gay fellatio and a three-way with a man and two women. The film's US distributor has even speculated that *Shame* may be the first NC-17 film that a larger audience will flock to, their attitudes having changed so much that they are no longer deterred by such a repressive rating: 'NC-17 is a badge of honour, not a scarlet letter. We believe it is time for the rating to become usable in a serious manner. ...The sheer talent of the actors and the vision of the filmmaker are extraordinary. ...It's a game changer.'[11]

In spite of these advances, there are still changes that have not been made and aspects of sexuality that remain under-represented, even in contemporary erotic cinema. Back in 1973, Norman Mailer recognised *Last Tango in Paris* as a breakthrough in its bold depiction of sex by two mainstream stars, Marlon Brando and Maria Schneider, but he also criticised the film for not being brave enough to go all the way: 'Brando's real cock up Schneider's real vagina would have brought the history of film one huge march closer to the ultimate experience it has promised since its inception (which is to re-embody life). ...We are being given a fuck film without the fuck. It is like a Western without the horses.'[12] Almost 40 years later, the closest cinema has come to unsimulated sex between two name actors is Kerry Fox and Mark Rylance in *Intimacy*, but they are not megastars and their contact stops at fellatio without going on to penetration. What we don't have are Brad Pitt and Angelina Jolie – or Kate Winslet and Leonardo DiCaprio – in a scene of actual intercourse. Rather than accepting sex organs and sexual relations as a natural – even wonderful – part of life and depicting these in mainstream movies with idealised stars, we continue to consign sex to porn films as if there were something dirty or shameful about the body and its desires. In the early '70s, 'porno chic' films like *Deep Throat* ('the world's first sexually explicit blockbuster') and *Behind the Green Door* ('an attempt to raise the pornographic film to the level of art')[13] seemed poised to bridge the gap between adult films and films for adults, between arse and art. As Paul Thomas Anderson (director of *Boogie Nights*) has said, 'Where I romanticise it could have gone was a place where acting, storytelling and camerawork got better. With interesting characters where you also had the luxury to show them fucking. We can't see Forrest Gump fuck Jenny Curran, to make that kid. But, God, wouldn't it be a great scene? Not just because I want to get off watching Tom Hanks fuck Robin Wright, but think what can be told about Gump through watching him have sex. ...My romantic notion is that if porno films had been allowed to breathe, and the stories eventually really did come first, then we would have been able to see an actor playing a role and then being able to try on a new way of having sex in a scene.'[14]

Besides the absence of big-name stars having real sex on screen, most erotic scenes in mainstream movies remain limited to a very narrow range of body-types and sexual situations. Lovers are usually white and young with model-perfect physiques. Desire is prompted by someone new, as in teens just discovering sex, a young couple making out on a first date or a youthful-looking married woman finding excitement in adultery. What you don't see are conjugal partners still overcome with carnal desire for each other and doing unspeakable things together in the marital bed. You don't see middle-aged or older couples with beer bellies or wrinkled faces engaged in sexual acts which show that extra flesh and a lived-in body can be arousing in themselves. That mole, pimple or scar – that asymmetrical breast or tiny penis – can inspire as much passion as the air-brushed and surgically corrected specimens normally on display. Androgynous bodies of males with full hips and females with small breasts, bodies of 'black' or 'red' or 'yellow' skin colour, differently abled bodies with certain heightened abilities and senses – the existing repertoire of erotic images could be expanded to include these. Instead of the usual vigorous thrusting, masculine tenderness could be shown as a turn-on, along with feminine sexual aggression. The tantalising feeling of barely touching – or sensing the air electrified with desire across the narrow gap separating a couple – is as sexy as going at it hot and heavy, yet such rarefied desire is rarely conveyed on film. The erotic dimensions of intellectual excitement or artistic expression or religious ecstasy are additional aspects of sexuality that could be explored on screen.

If the range of bodies we see making love could be greatly expanded beyond the presently impoverished view, so too could the body itself be opened up to enjoyment in ways beyond those in which the current cinema has 'zoned' it for pleasure. The hollow of the neck, the crook of the arm, and the back of the knee are all potential erogenous zones, readily responding to touch and, if stimulated, capable of inflaming the whole body. Though film is a visual medium, close-ups of a hand stroking skin can evoke a tactile response in the viewer. Beard, chest, underarm and pubic hair excite nerve endings when stroked and are near sweat glands which the nose can find arousing. Yet, rather than focus on hair, film usually ignores or passes quickly over it – a glimpse of underarm, a flash of pubes – to get to the genitals. What you hear endless dialogue about – and occasionally actually see – in mainstream sex scenes are the penis and the vagina. However, virtually no attention is paid to the clitoris, despite the fact that stimulation of it is the surest way for most women to achieve orgasm. Is this because the clit is often 'hidden' under a hood when not erect, or because a too-tight close-up of it would be 'obscene' – or just because cinema remains largely sexist in disregarding female pleasure? Shots of vigorous thrusting remain the norm, whether or not these make contact with the clitoris or the G-spot. Most sex scenes are phallocentric: she is expected to come from what stimulates him, from the thrusts we can see and not from some organ we can't. This phallocentrism also means that the man's testicles are entirely overlooked as a potential means of pleasure. Made to perform a largely symbolic function (a film character with 'big balls' is potently dominant), the testicles are deprived of their physical presence and sensual capacity. The camera so rarely shows them, it's as though they aren't even there! Similarly, for both men and women, the ass and the anus have very little sensual presence in current cinema. They are a source of humorous embarrassment for men (when caught with their pants down in sex comedies) and of teasing foreplay on the part of women (who may flash their backsides as a lure to vaginal intercourse). But mainstream film almost never shows the ass or anus as exciting in themselves, despite the latter's lasciviously sensitive nerve endings and the fact that anal intercourse can stimulate the prostate and the clitoris.

Although it doesn't always go far enough in certain directions, one trend in contemporary erotic cinema is clearly towards an increasing liberalisation of sexual attitudes. However, there is a significant counter-trend which explores the question of whether some limits on sexual gratification may be advisable and even necessary. In the age of AIDS, can someone who is HIV-positive have unprotected sex with a partner (*The Living End*) or not even tell about his HIV status (*Savage Nights*)?

Is the ideal really an absolute instinctual freedom in which anything goes? Should nothing be taboo? What about incest (*Lolita*) or bestiality (*Zoo*) or necrophilia (*Kissed*)? How about sado-masochistic sex that borders on rape (*A History of Violence*) or that could result in injury or death (*Killing Me Softly*)? Unbridled desire can lead a mother to endanger her young son (*Little Children*) or cause a father to steal his grown son's fiancée, exposing him to a killing shock (*Damage*). Lust can provoke a teenage girl to fellate a series of anonymous men (*Melissa P*) or a husband to force his wife into a three-way that includes double penetration (*The Ages of Lulú*). According to director Jean-Claude Brisseau, whose female characters in *The Exterminating Angels* become sensation-seekers compelled to engage in ever-more extreme sexual experiences, 'I am mostly and quite frankly in favour of the liberalisation and acceptance of a whole series of things in the sexual domain. These women cross a barrier. But this barrier, it will forever recede. The more they transgress taboos, the more frustrated they'll get because there will always be a stronger taboo, up to the point of death.' Brisseau adds that 'This is what happens to all libertines, who end up no longer capable of orgasm because they can never reach the ultimate taboo, except in death. ...I remember the rather poignant confession of a man, a true libertine, who told me: "I've gone through all the stages. First I made love with a woman, then with two, then three, then I moved on to men, and now I've become a sado-masochist. So, the last pleasure that remains for me is to hang myself by the balls."'[15]

The hedonistic male character in *Shame* ends up in a similar downward spiral of ever-more degrading lust – an unchecked carnality which is not coincidentally fuelled by his constant consumption of porn. It is quite striking how many contemporary films show the sexual revolution as having been co-opted by porn, which holds out the promise of libidinal freedom only to trap the consumer into a never-satisfied demand for more extreme images of pre-packaged lust. What looks like liberation becomes a new kind of conformity to capitalism, a 'repressive desublimation' in which individual instinct doesn't find healthy release but is instead channelled into the false freedom of porn-dictated desire. *All About Anna*, *The Brown Bunny*, *The Centre of the World*, *Destricted*, *Enter the Void*, *The Fluffer* – these are just some of the most recent films to critically examine the effect of pornography on the contemporary libido and to suggest that, despite – or maybe because of – liberalisation, sex still isn't free.

EROTIC GENRES

ANIMATION

Heavy Metal 2000 (2000)

Directors: Michael Coldewey, Michel Lemire
Voice Cast: Julie Strain (Julie)

Animators can reshape the sexual body beyond the limits of the live-action human form. In this science-fiction/fantasy film, a street vendor offers a Cyber Sex Doll equipped with every imaginable feature: 'We're talking high-grade silicone rubber flesh here and a PVC skeleton with plastic ball-and-socket joints for optimum movement. You can customise her with a choice of seven synthetic hair dyes and optional entry ports with four speeds of suction. She's loaded with the latest microsensor orgasmatronic technology and an expandable vocabulary of over 200 dirty words.' As the sexbot pulls a male customer to her breasts, she coos enticingly, 'Please select your sexual preference: vaginal, anal, oral, other.' Given this ability to morph into a nearly limitless range of sexual options to serve the customer's desire, is it any wonder that 'test results indicate she's better than the real thing'?

But the interesting point is that she's not. Despite the sales talk (and the accompanying heavy-metal song – 'She can sense the pervert inside of me/She knows how to make me howl'), the Cyber Sex Doll is depicted as a debased female brought to her knees, with her arms together in front of her as if chained. She is dominated by the obese, one-eyed pimp who holds her down, hawking her as merchandise. Her male customer is fascinated but also frightened by the big silicone breasts she pulls him into – as if the overabundance of choice were too much, the satisfaction of his desire too rotely mechanical, based too strongly on what he is conditioned to want, on what is sold to him. When the pimp then offers him a 'Fillacian blowfish' as an alternative, with its connotations of fellatio and poison, it's clear that the moviemakers, while excited by a sucking mouth (a sexbot's or a fish's), also sense that such mechanical or bestial sex would be a kind of death. Julie, the film's heroine, calls the male a 'sick, twisted, low-life, scum-sucking pig' for being attracted to such inferior substitutes for human females as herself. Later, as the Cyber Sex Doll emits orgasmic cries and contorts its limbs in climactic convulsions, Julie shoots it to put it out of its misery, for it is nothing but a robot gone haywire: all it can achieve is a soulless mechanical imitation of human ecstasy.

Curiously, the character of Julie is voiced by and modelled on Julie Strain, a *Penthouse* model and B-movie actress famous for her big – and silicone-enhanced – breasts. In fact, Strain is one of the featured interview subjects in the documentary *Boobs: An American Obsession* (2010). A significant amount of attention is paid to Julie's breasts in *Heavy Metal 2000*, such as in the scene where she dons unusual body 'armour': a one-piece combination of red thong and ripped, form-fitting leotard top. The film celebrates the power of Julie's natural and human female sexuality – ignoring the extent to which she herself is an artificially enhanced and commodified body-type.

Team America: World Police (2004)

Director: Trey Parker
Voice Cast: Trey Parker (Gary), Kristen Miller (Lisa)

Should puppet sex be rated NC-17? The lovemaking between Gary and Lisa in this film is enacted entirely by puppets whose strings are visible and who are not anatomically correct (they have no genitals). Yet the film had to be submitted nine times to the MPAA ratings board, which kept demanding further cuts before they would grant it an R rating. According to director Trey Parker – co-creator along with Matt Stone of the *South Park* TV series and the film *South Park: Bigger, Longer & Uncut* (1999) – 'It was all about the sexual positions.' At times, it seemed as though these 'couldn't be anything but missionary'.[16] In the uncut version of the film, Gary and Lisa do engage in a variety of sexual positions and acts, including cowgirl and reverse cowgirl; 69ing and cunnilingus from behind; rear entry and/or anal; urination and defecation; and possibly foot fetishism. (The R-rated version drastically shortens most of these and deletes the scatology.) Parker felt that the ratings board didn't seem to get that this was a *comedy*: 'It's something we all did as kids with Barbie and Ken dolls. ...The whole joke of it is that it's just two dolls flopping around on each other. You see the hinges on their legs.'[17] Of course, it's possible that the association with child sex-play made the 'doll sex' seem even more obscene, as infantile sexuality and polymorphous perversity tend to make many people uncomfortable.

The puppet sex scene is actually a parody of the love scenes that are interspersed with the patriotic violence in Jerry Bruckheimer action/adventure films like *Top Gun* (1986), *Armageddon* (1998) and *Pearl Harbor* (2001). Gary and Lisa are members of an American paramilitary force fighting global terrorism, a group that 'naïvely' tends to destroy villages – like Paris and Cairo – in the process of saving them. The scene begins as a candle-lit romantic encounter between two clean-cut kids with the Gary and Lisa dolls falling onto the bed in slow motion and gazing into each other's eyes. She strokes his manly chest and we see a cuddly shot of their legs and feet intertwined. But then, as the two assume the various positions and run through all the acts (including intercourse while she does a headstand), the sex becomes less about kindred spirits and more about gymnastic bodies, a parody of American athleticism and 'healthy' libido, as superficial and mechanical as illustrations in a *Joy of Sex* how-to manual. Within this 'American innocence' lurks something dark and perverse, as revealed by his increasingly violent rear entry, her devouring of his cock and their pissing and shitting on each other. Like US patriotism, American sex is satirised as having a violent underside.

A Scanner Darkly (2006)

Director: Richard Linklater
Cast: Keanu Reeves (Bob/Fred), Winona Ryder (Donna/Hank), Lisa Marie Newmyer (Connie)

Bob and Donna seem to have a deep emotional connection, but she won't sleep with him. So Bob takes drugs and has sex with a substitute, Connie. Afterwards, he briefly sees Donna's face instead of Connie's on the woman lying next to him. Later, Bob, who is actually an undercover narc named Fred, watches surveillance video of himself and Connie in bed. As the tape fast-forwards, the two are seen moving rapidly through various sexual positions. Theirs is a merely physical encounter, a mechanical conjoining of bodies like the speeded-up sex between Alex (Malcolm McDowell) and the two girls in *A Clockwork Orange* (1971). But Bob then projects one segment of his own sex scene as a hologram, focusing in on one freeze-framed image that indeed seems to show that Connie has morphed into Donna! Did

Bob actually have sex with the woman he loves but not really experience it because he was so addled by drugs – or so alienated by his duplicitous role as a narc, always spying on others and himself like a voyeur at a porn film of his own life?

The characters in *A Scanner Darkly* were created by filming live actors and then having animators use a rotoscopic computer program to hand-draw over each frame of the actors' images. Thus each character looks like something of a blur of unstable boundaries and multiple superimpositions, as if seen through a drug haze or in video-scan mode. The animation itself dramatises the sense in which video or drugs perhaps allow Bob to imagine being with his beloved Donna, while they actually impede any real connection. As he tries to identify his female bed-partner in the surveillance video, Bob is wearing a futuristic 'scramble suit' that hides his own identity from others by rapidly morphing his image into a blur of different faces and body-types. How can Bob find love if he is losing touch with who he himself is? The 'scramble suit' is a metaphor for Bob's schizophrenia (is he addict or narc? Bob or Fred?). Fred apparently left a happy home with a loving wife because he was bored with suburbia, feeling that 'nothing would ever change', but now as an undercover cop suffering from dissociative disorder, Fred/Bob finds that everything is changing all the time, with love a mere sexual performance. Even his boss at police headquarters, Hank, is revealed to be Donna in a 'scramble suit', who has been manipulating Fred/Bob into unwittingly taking on an undercover assignment in which he could lose his mind forever. Has the beloved become a femme fatale or is this just another of Fred/Bob's imaginings, such as the one where a one-night-stand became the woman of his dreams?

COMEDY

Porky's (1982)

Director: Bob Clark
Cast: Kaki Hunter (Wendy), Wyatt Knight (Tommy), Dan Monahan (Pee Wee), Nancy Parsons (Miss Balbricker)

This coming-of-age sex comedy, set in 1950s' Florida, is notorious for the scene in which three high-school boys peer through peepholes at girls in the shower room after gym class. At first the humour would seem to be at the girls' expense as they are unwittingly caught naked by the boys' prying eyes. 'This has got to be the biggest beaver shoot in the history of Florida,' the boys joke to one another, viewing the girls as objects of an animal hunt and a sex film (and making us aware of ourselves as voyeurs of this 'sex film' called *Porky's*). However, when the peeping Toms are discovered, the girls – who cover up with towels but do not seem terribly embarrassed – turn *their* eyes on the boys. Says Wendy to Tommy about his spying friend, 'If Pee Wee's with you, you better cover his eyes; he might get confused.' As with the belittling nickname 'Pee Wee', Wendy implies that one of the boys is too young to understand what he is seeing – too small for sex. A mini-war for gender dominance ensues, with Tommy talking dirty and sticking his tongue through the hole, Wendy slathering suds on it (as if to tell him to wash his mouth out with soap) and Tommy then poking his penis through. This virile display seems to rout Wendy, who runs away from the shower wall to shudder and scream with the other girls, but theirs are shrieks of delight more than fear, and Tommy's own laugh is one of mutual enjoyment and not just macho triumph. Tommy waggles his male member and makes it talk in a little boy's voice in a gesture that combines phallic aggression with childlike innocence: 'Hi, I'm Paulie the Penis and I just love to have fun!' The girls look eager to stay and play, but at this point their gym teacher Miss Balbricker catches sight of the offending member and grabs hold of it as it protrudes through the shower wall. As director Bob Clark notes, the ratings board made him delete shots of the (fake) penis, but 'in the real movie, before I had to do some cutting, Miss Balbricker had a hold of it' with 'both her feet up against the wall. Just the penis was holding her up. It was the funniest thing I think I've ever seen.'[18] Here the joke is on the adult authority-figure so manically repressive of teen sexuality that she nearly dismembers the boy, while her penis envy and her underlying desire for the male sex are also revealed. At the same time, the joke is on the teenage boy for being so proud of his manhood and so sexually aggressive that he practically tempts (a feminist) fate to castrate him. As Clark has said, 'All the women, they were in control, not the men; the men were always running around with their penises hanging out, looking like fools.'[19]

American Pie (1999)

Director: Paul Weitz
Cast: Jason Biggs (the boy Jim), Eugene Levy (the father), Molly Cheek (the mother)

Few scenes in sex comedies are as infamous as the one that gives this film its title, in which a father arrives home unexpectedly to find his teenage son humping a warm apple pie – a freshly baked treat left out for the boy by his mother. Why has this scene become such a hilarious highlight? First, there is the fact of the boy, in his sexual ignorance, taking his friends' words *literally*. Earlier, when he asked 'what exactly does third base feel like?' they told him 'like warm apple pie'. Second, there is the idea of a hormonally driven teen so desperate for sex that he feels compelled to screw a pastry. Even his father, though admitting to similar urges, says that he 'never did it with baked goods'. Third, the boy is caught with his pants down in the incriminating act by his own father and is thus exposed as vulnerable to paternal punishment. However, part of the scene's good-natured humour is that the dad is understanding and actually proves to be the boy's ally, complicit in a cover-up of the illicit act: 'We'll just tell your mother that we ate it all.' Finally, it is his own mother's pie that the boy gets down and dirty with. He profanes her sweet innocence with his 'depravity', as if coming close to violating the incest taboo. (Elsewhere in the film, one of this boy's buddies actually sleeps with a friend's mother.) And then there is that expression 'as American as Mom and apple pie'. It is almost as though, in his selfish lust, the boy 'desecrates' his dear mom, his happy home and his entire beloved country. As director Paul Weitz has noted, 'In the States, with the apple-pie family and all the baggage that goes with that concept, a kid with his dick in an apple pie is really quite an aggressively subversive image'.[20] But the humour also works the other way, bringing 'dirty' masturbation into the maternal home, fostering a warm acceptance of teen desires that in past years would have been condemned as merely 'depraved'. In this sense, *American Pie* is one of the sweetest sex comedies – especially this scene with the pie.

Another funny aspect of this film is its ridiculous battle with the MPAA over this scene. In the unrated version, the boy is lying on top of the kitchen counter and working the pie with missionary zeal. However, as in the old censor's rule that lovers had to keep at least one foot on the floor in any bedroom scene lest the action get too steamy, the ratings board preferred that the boy remain vertical with the pie. So, in the R-rated version, the boy stands with his back to us, humping the pie up against the kitchen counter. This does set up what is perhaps an even more obscene sight gag: when discovered by his father, the boy turns around to reveal the pie at his crotch. As the boy lifts his hands away, the pie stays up without his having to hold onto it! The ratings board also insisted on a reduction in the number of pie-thrusts – as if that really made the scene any less offensive to those inclined to be offended: 'The MPAA was like "Can he thrust two times instead of four?"'[21]

HORROR

Nekromantik (1987)

Director: Jörg Buttgereit
Cast: Daktari Lorenz (Rob), Beatrice Manowski (Betty)

Rob works on a cleaning crew that collects the remains of accident or murder victims. Sometimes he returns to his apartment with organs and body parts, which he preserves in jars of formaldehyde. One day he brings home a man's corpse, and Rob and his girlfriend Betty engage in a *ménage à trois* with it. She rides a broken-off broom handle protruding from the corpse's crotch while Rob has sex with her from behind. Rob kisses the cadaver's mouth before Betty's and then moves its skeletal hand to feel up her breast. The scene is filmed romantically, using soft focus, slow motion and piano music. Is there any point to this necrophilia other than to disturb viewers of this horror film? Is Rob really in love with death?

One clue to an answer can be found in the scene where Rob dissects and disembowels a cadaver, which is cross-cut with a memory of 'Rob's father, killing his son's favourite pet'[22] – a rabbit that has its throat slit and its body gutted. This flashback was 'triggered by a programme on TV' about phobias,[23] such as an aversion to spiders, dirt, excrement or dead bodies, which can perhaps be cured 'when the person is continually confronted with' the phobic object. The young Rob, traumatised by the death of his pet rabbit with which he seems to identify, tries to deal with this trauma by acting as a 'pathologist' and thus adopting the position of his father as a knife-wielding killer. Rob's preservation of dead body parts shows his fixation on the gutted rabbit. Rob tries to overcome his fear of death by continually confronting himself with corpses, moving from a frightening identification with the dead to the triumphant mastery of a murderer. This is why the sex is a three-way: Rob is both the corpse of the man being laid and his live self doing the laying, as he moves from being 'fucked' by death to being the 'fucker'.

Unfortunately, this means that Rob cannot have reciprocal relations with a woman. Sex for him must always be mediated by murder; the only way he can 'love' Betty is to imagine mastering death through her, as when he 'fucks' her as she rides the corpse. Rob needs to feel like a killer in order to get turned on, as when his hand uses the corpse's hand to maul her breast. Later, after Betty leaves him, Rob finds that he cannot get it up with a prostitute until he strangles her in a cemetery, after which he is able to sexually dominate her dead body. Ultimately, though, no amount of lust-murder can help Rob get over that gutted rabbit. In the end, the only way he can think to make things right (he imagines the rabbit-gutting run in reverse so that the animal is again alive and whole) is to plunge a knife repeatedly into his own belly, which results in ejaculations of semen and then blood. In this way, Rob is at once killer-father and killed rabbit, resolving the split in his psyche through a suicidal *Liebestod*. Like the figure of Christ he nails to a cross, Rob atones for his and his father's murderous sins by sacrificing himself.

Ginger Snaps (2000)

Director: John Fawcett
Cast: Emily Perkins (Brigitte), Katharine Isabelle (Ginger), Mimi Rogers (their mother), Jesse Moss (Jason), Kris Lemche (Sam)

In this hormonal horror film, lycanthropy is a figure for teenage fears of puberty and sexuality. Ginger can't understand why others aren't horrified by the changes in her body – the blood, back pain and hair growth that mark the 'curse' of her sexual development. To her, menstruation itself is monstrous. Her sister Brigitte is equally horrified by Ginger's sudden bloodlust for boys, who wolf-whistle at her and hunger for her sex. The two goth girls had made a pact that they would die before succumbing to men and becoming a gender stereotype like their mother, a suburban housewife. But now, after being bitten by a werewolf and having her first menses on a night with a full moon, Ginger starts toking on a joint offered to her by football jock Jason, and Brigitte fears that next her sister will be 'sucking [him] off'.

Yet Ginger's physical transformation makes her into something ambiguously other than a subservient woman, as evidenced by the fact that she sprouts a tail which at first looks like a large clitoris but then grows longer than a penis. When Jason takes her for sex in the backseat of his car, she is the aggressive one. Refusing to 'lie back and relax', to let him be 'the guy' or to use 'protection', she pushes him back, tears open his clothes and devours him. Rather than be victimised by male lust, she herself preys upon and eventually kills a series of men.

While Ginger describes this killing in terms of sexual self-empowerment ('It feels so good. It's like touching yourself. ...I'm a goddamn force of nature!'), the masturbation metaphor suggests her narcissistic disregard for others. Brigitte feels that Ginger has gone too far in giving Jason her disease ('You had unprotected sex and you infected him') and in becoming a man-hater and a man-eater. Brigitte attempts to cure her sister of lycanthropy by piercing her navel with a silver ring, as if either goth-girl rebellion or heterosexual marriage might serve as an antidote to actual man-slaughter. When this fails, Brigitte has her friend Sam try to spring upon Ginger with a hypodermic needle and inject a cure, but rather than surrender to this kind of phallic force, the she-wolf Ginger attacks Sam and tries to get Brigitte to join her in drinking the boy's blood. In sisterly solidarity, Brigitte tries but vomits, unable to do it. When Ginger then attacks her, Brigitte ends up stabbing her with a knife in self-defence. In a sense, Brigitte sides with patriarchal society, using phallic violence to put down Ginger's unruly female sexuality. To Brigitte, the pact the sisters had made to avoid heterosexual conformity has indeed come to seem like suicide, associated with things that she – like society – now fears: narcissism, lesbianism, incest and death. And yet Brigitte holds Ginger in a loving embrace as she dies, perhaps realising that the rebellious part of herself is dying along with her sister.

Teeth (2007)

Director: Mitchell Lichtenstein
Cast: Jess Weixler (Dawn), John Hensley (Brad)

As a boy, Brad plays a game of 'I'll show you mine if you show me yours' with his younger stepsister Dawn. He fondles her and has his finger bitten by the teeth in her vagina (or at least he imagines that this is what happens). He represses this traumatic event, but it has an unconscious influence on his psychosexual development in the years to come. On the one hand, castration anxiety leads Brad to avoid vaginal intercourse and to insist on rough anal and oral sex with his girlfriend, as if punishing her for the past injury he received from a female. On the other hand, that injury seems to have eroticised being bitten in Brad's mind, so that even oral sex becomes a flirtation with danger. Obsessed with teeth, Brad is almost bitten by his female dog after playing with her, and he tries to push a dog-biscuit bone into his girlfriend's mouth, revealing her incisors. 'You look a lot better with a dick in your mouth,' Brad tells her, both avoiding – and indirectly approaching – the *vagina dentata*. Sex has become sado-masochistic for Brad; fear of, and violence against, the female make it exciting.

However, there is also the persistent sense of an injured childhood innocence and an underlying hope for love. Brad says that he has always loved his stepsister Dawn and believes that *she* has been saving herself for *him*. When they do end up in bed together, he first moves to take her anally, but she lifts her nightgown to show him her vagina and he seems pacified, as if finally granted the reassuring sight of her that he wanted as a little boy. He enters her, saying 'We always knew it'd play out this way eventually, didn't we, ever since we were little kids?' It would seem that Brad has come full circle, having finally conquered his childish fear of the female sex as a castrated and castrating difference. (Since the little girl doesn't have a penis, does this mean that she lost hers and could take his?) However, as Brad's finger traces the lips around Dawn's mouth near her teeth, he flashes back to the (imagined?) time when her toothed vagina first bit him, and he groans as he feels (or imagines?) his penis being chomped off below. It is as though Brad's fears get the better of him, making his destiny one that climaxes in sado-masochistic death rather than in loving acceptance of the other sex. Instead of conquering his own gynophobia, Brad falls victim to the male myth of the *vagina dentata*: 'The myth springs from a primitive masculine dread of the mysteries of women and sexual union – fears of weakness, impotence. It is a nightmare image of the power and horror of female sexuality.'

MOVIES ABOUT MOVIES

The Fluffer (2001)

Directors: Richard Glatzer, Wash Westmoreland
Cast: Scott Gurney (Johnny), Michael Cunio (Sean)

After falling for a male porn star he sees in a gay video, Sean goes on to become a cameraman and then a fluffer on the studio set. Each new job is ostensibly one step closer to his porn idol, Johnny Rebel, but in fact they all allow Sean to maintain a similar kind of psychosexual distance. Johnny is viewed as an idealised image of macho glamour as close-ups fetishise his muscled torso and his extensive hard-on. However, the glass TV screen and the camera lens also separate Sean from the very man they offer to him as the object of his sexual fantasies. Similarly, while fluffing may seem to bring Sean up-close and personal to his idol Johnny, the fact that it is a paid job on a porn set – fellating the performer to make him erect – creates a professional barrier to intimacy, making it more about money and meat than romance. Sean is on his knees before Johnny's cock on the video screen and on the porn set, worshipping him as a sex god, obsessed with him because such perfectly pumped maleness is unattainable. And Sean wants Johnny not in spite of the fact that the latter is apparently straight but *because* of it; Sean's desire is fed by what he cannot have. When he was young, Sean used to take photos of a studly straight man who, after having sex with the boy, abandoned him, causing him to feel that it was his fault. Sean's first sexual experience thus imprinted on him a worship of elusive hetero masculinity and a feeling of his own inferiority and guilt. Sean's abject adoration of his porn idol Johnny is a kind of masochistic relationship: 'In my mind, I'll always be on my knees in front of him.'

But what Sean really desires in Johnny is the image of someone who feels good about himself as a man and is proud to show it. This is the real reason Sean is so impressed with Johnny as a porn star; he imagines him as someone who has so overcome his guilt that he can exhibit his manhood and unabashedly engage in (gay) sex the way Sean wishes he could. 'It must be tough having sex in front of all these people,' Sean comments on set and Johnny replies, 'No, I could do it in front of an Olympic stadium, man.' The 'O' on the shirt that Sean wears in this scene is a sign of his zero self-worth and his open-mouthed admiration for Johnny, but it is also an indication that the oral fluffing Sean gives him is deep down a desire for a real connection – to be recognised as, and not just taken by, a man.

The Pornographer (Le pornographe) (2001)

Director: Bertrand Bonello
Cast: Jean-Pierre Léaud (Jacques), Ovidie (the actress)

Can porn be art? Jacques made innovative porn films in the 1970s as part of the sexual revolution. Now he's trying to make a comeback but finds himself constantly deflated by a commercially minded producer who insists on utter conventionality. During the filming of one sex scene, the producer wrests directorial control from Jacques and imposes all the standard rules so that everything becomes blandly generic. Canned music is played and potted flowers are brought in for 'erotic' ambiance. The actress is to wear 'alluring' nail polish; she must emit 'impassioned' moans. The 'lovers' must go through the motions of assuming all the expected sexual positions with close-ups of their organs and orifices, and the scene must climax in a money shot of him ejaculating onto her face. Seeing this, Jacques droops his head, for he is seeking the more elevated excitement of something unpotted and unpolished, a passion that isn't already pre-packaged by capitalism.

As director Bertrand Bonello explains, 'the question "Can one make a beautiful porn scene?" then became "Can one change the codes?"'[24] This is what Jacques tries to do: through 'the framing' which 'plac[es] them at a distance' so that they become humans interacting and not just interlocking body parts, and through 'the editing', which makes them less fragmented. Then, at the climax, Jacques 'seeks to film the ejaculation in an intimate way, without the final explosion in her face. But, in a porn film, that's impossible. Because if the ejaculation isn't shown, there is nothing. It's a little like the gunshot in a western's final duel: it marks the end of the scene.'[25]

Implicit in Bonello's comment is the idea that most sex in porn is like a duel which the man wins by 'shooting' into the woman's face, with his pleasure triumphing over hers. By contrast, Jacques had wanted to see *her* pleasure. He considers 'the face' to be 'the last bastion of humanity' and says about another actress that 'when she comes at the end, I was almost in tears as I shot the scene. In my films, there's always something beautiful, even if you find the rest terribly ugly. Why? Because it's pure, raw sex and therefore profoundly human.' Jacques would strip the sex scene of all its artificial trappings and commercial codes. He would purify it of everything that makes it seem like 'dirty' porn. The resulting concentration on raw flesh, on the body seen, would paradoxically enable him to move beyond mere porn, to access unseen (female) pleasure – not just the physical discharge of an ejaculating organ but the ecstasy of feeling implied by a face. And so, in the porn film that Jacques dreams of making about a fox hunt where a woman is the prey, the emphasis is not on the climax where the men 'shoot' but rather on their pursuit of the female, whose pleasure eludes their attempts to capture it. The tired porn scenario of a fox hunt is merely a means to something beyond. It is a search to film real feeling, to make porn into art.

Zack and Miri Make a Porno (2008)

Director: Kevin Smith
Cast: Seth Rogen (Zack), Elizabeth Banks (Miri)

Zack and Miri, friends since first grade, are 20-something roommates who 'really do know too much about each other'. She knows, for example, that he's interested in buying a 'pocket pussy' sex toy, which she mocks: '"Real feel action" – oh, my God!' He knows that she uses a dildo because, as she explains, 'I never met a man who can make me come like a vibrator does.' Each is disgusted by the other's recourse to mechanical substitutes for sex, and yet they joke about it in grudging recognition of a common need. Their raunchy humour is itself a kind of substitute, allowing them to turn each other on but deny that it is anything truly sensual or serious.

One day, when Zack catches a teen voyeur taking cam-phone footage of Miri in her underwear, Zack blocks the view by mooning the camera. His instinct is to protect her from prying eyes, not to see her as a sex object, but this very act also allows him to take down his pants and 'cover' her body with his, surreptitiously satisfying another instinct. When a viral video of their backsides shows up on YouTube – captioned 'My name's Granny Panties and nobody wants to fuck me' and 'Nothing's whiter than my big gay ass' – they are both embarrassed at the public exposure, which ridicules them as unattractive (at least in the conventional sense of not being younger or slimmer). Yet this laying bare of insecurities helps them to overcome shame and to laugh at their flaws, and the fact that her underwear and his ass become famous as web images ironically helps them to accept their bodies despite the mockery.

The web video also gives Zack and Miri the idea to make an amateur porn movie to pay off some debts. As a way of insisting that it will be nothing but meaningless sex, Zack pitches the project as a mock marriage proposal ('Miriam Linky, will you have sex with me on camera?'), but the metaphor suggests the underlying solemnity of the occasion and already implies that love will be a part of the sex act as it occurs in front of public 'witnesses'. Indeed, when the two do act in their amateur sex scene, the video crew is the first to recognise true feeling and has to show Zack footage of himself with Miri for *him* to realise it. These two would never have had the courage to come together were it not just a jokey porn film, but once they are in the scene they cannot pretend that the sex is only for show. 'Let me see them titties!' Zack orders but then covers Miri's breasts to keep her from exposing them to anyone else. The two have sex fully clothed, with the camera focused on their faces – a decision which director Kevin Smith made and communicated to actors Seth Rogen (Zack) and Elizabeth Banks (Miri) only at the last minute: 'If... we see Seth's ass', it 'will make people laugh', or if 'we see [her] tits', it will just make people think "We've finally seen Elizabeth Banks' tits".[26] More than viewers of a comedy or voyeurs of porn, we are witnesses to love in the end.

PORN

Deep Throat (1972)

Director: Gerard Damiano
Cast: Linda Lovelace (Herself), Dolly Sharp (Helen), Harry Reems (Dr Young)

Is this pioneering hardcore film about *female* pleasure as much as male? At first it may seem so, as Linda comes home to find her roommate Helen with her legs spread on the kitchen table while a man gives her cunnilingus. However, Helen seems bored by the act, asking him 'Do you mind if I smoke while you're eating?' and then appearing to enjoy the cigarette in her mouth more than his tongue on her clit. Already the film seems to be preparing us for a male doctor's later 'revelation' that Linda's clitoris is in her throat and that her pleasure must therefore be found in fellating men. Helen had encouraged Linda to find her own way to sexual satisfaction apart from the 'wham bam thank you ma'am' path taken by many men, and certainly women can get pleasure from giving head (*Deep Throat* is said to have inspired a great deal of exciting experimentation along these lines), but the idea that Linda can only orgasm this way makes her dependent on the male member and denies her the pleasure of her actual clitoris below. According to feminist Erica Jong, 'Men want to believe that the clitoris is in a woman's throat because... then they can believe that by thrusting their penis into a woman's mouth, she gets as much pleasure as they do. Guess what? It's not true.'[27] This notion of Linda's 'oral orgasm' would seem to be more of a male fantasy, as is perhaps indicated by the *phallic* imagery – the thrusting rocket launch and the firework bombs bursting – used to symbolise *her* climax.

The fantasy may originate in male anxiety over a woman's actual clitoris being too much like a penis. 'You don't have one,' says the doctor examining Linda between her legs, and her reply – 'Well, I'm a woman; I'm not supposed to have one' – is precisely to the point: it is reassuring for him to think that she doesn't have a clitoris or anything else resembling a penis down there. *He* is the one with the phallus. Male anxieties are further overcome at the end when a short, nebbishy guy proves to have a 13-inch cock that thoroughly satisfies Linda's oral cravings. Thus, her 'oral orgasm' turns out to be more about *his* size and potency. Her fulfilment is the background to *his* satisfaction.

Behind the Green Door (1972)

Directors: Mitchell Brothers (Artie Mitchell, Jim Mitchell)
Cast: Marilyn Chambers (Gloria), Johnny Keyes (Stud), George S MacDonald (Barry)

Two kidnappers (played by this film's co-directors!) take Gloria to a private club, where a female attendant gives her a whole-body massage and then several women work on her together, kissing, stroking and licking her. Gloria is apparently rather uptight and frigid, and these women help her to 'relax' and get 'warm'. They serve to transition Gloria gently into sensuality, almost as though the women were an extension of her own self-pleasuring. Rather than being seen as fulfilling in itself, lesbianism becomes a kind of auto-eroticism and a mere warm-up for the heterosexual act to follow. After being stripped of her white gown and laid spread-eagled on a bed before a viewing audience, Gloria is then penetrated by a black man who wears face paint and a bone necklace. This scene of a 'virgin' being sacrificed to an 'African savage' suggests that a little violence is needed to break through Gloria's inhibitions and divulge her 'primitive' sexuality. The film doesn't want us to see this as a rape but as an unconsciously desired sexual awakening, a ritual 'ravishment' where Gloria is shocked into responsiveness and where her 'tortured' reactions are due only to sexual repression which eventually turns to orgasmic expression.

Marilyn Chambers, the actress playing Gloria, was best known as the 'pure' girl from Ivory Snow soap commercials. When we see this clean-cut blonde subjected to 'dirty' sex with a black 'savage', the film uses racist fear to incite lust. The size of the African-American's penis is emphasised by the fact that it protrudes from the cut-out crotch of his white tights, and the black/white contrast between him and her is made apparent in penetration shots and in those where the back of his dark head and shoulders obscures her face as he 'dominates' her. The audience in the club who are watching this white woman being 'taken' may want to rescue her, but they are told that they are 'powerless to stop the performance' and so should 'just relax and enjoy' themselves. The audience members are thus absolved of any guilt they may feel over miscegenous sex and freed to indulge in fantasies of superior black potency and white female ravishment.

Both this potency and this ravishment are intensified in the fantasy that follows, where Gloria simultaneously fellates one man and masturbates two others with her hands while riding the penis of a further man beneath her, even as several female attendants also get into the act with their hands and mouths. It is as though the multiplication of male organs and female orifices, combined with the magnification of these in close-up, is an attempt to figure the epitome of pleasure, the *ne plus ultra* of sexual ecstasy. At the climax, the various ejaculating penises and arcing drops of semen falling toward Gloria's face are presented as a kaleidoscopic, colour-negative special effect in optically printed slow motion. Orgiastic sex has reached such intensity that it becomes abstract, pure energy beyond bodies or organs.

But this is too extreme for your average American audience. A truck driver named Barry, who has been watching the scene as a member of the audience, suddenly takes conventionally manly action: he leaps up, extricates Gloria from the tangle of bodies and carries her out of the sex club. The two then proceed to have straight, white, monogamous sex – perhaps fuelled by the fantasy whose danger he just rescued her from?

The Devil in Miss Jones (1973)

Director: Gerard Damiano
Cast: Georgina Spelvin (Miss Jones)

Miss Jones is a virginal spinster who commits suicide in despair over her loneliness. Distressed when informed that she's going to Hell merely for having taken her own life, she asks to be allowed to commit some sins of lust so that she will truly deserve damnation. In one nude scene, she bites into an apple. She also holds a snake, flicking her tongue at it as it does likewise to her and putting its head into her mouth and its tail between her legs. Is she Eve seduced by the serpent-Devil into sex, or does Miss Jones already have the Devil inside her and is expressing her own sexual desires? Director Gerard Damiano said at the time of the film's release, 'The movies have been masculine fantasies up to now, exploiting women because you played to the male audience. But the audience today includes women, and I consider *Miss Jones* a totally feminine film. It's the males who become meat, reduced to objects of her fantasy. And it's the penis she's in love with, not the man.'[28]

While it's liberating to see women portrayed as desiring subjects, the reduction of men to sex objects may be less so. It seems more like reverse sexism ('You say we're cunts; well, you're a bunch of pricks!') or like aggrandisement of the male organ. 'It's getting so big, so hard,' Miss Jones says during a fellatio scene. 'It's like a tower, a beautiful tower. ...I can feel the life, the strength, the power. I must have that power. I must have you inside.' Certainly, a woman can find a man's size and strength exciting, but this cock worship is a bit over the top, and it seems alarmingly predicated on female lack: her weakness *needs* his strength. Indeed, the film's idea of Hell for Miss Jones is to have her masturbating in sexual frustration while pleading with a man who shows no interest in her, 'Would you put your cock in me? Then I can get off. I can't do it by myself. Damn you!' (In semi-Sartrean fashion, Hell is other people – who won't help you get off.) Apparently, director Damiano can't – or won't – see that Miss Jones doesn't need a man for her to get off; she could orgasm on her own from that masturbation.

Does the film really attend to *female* pleasure? During the anal sex scene, the pain on Miss Jones's face quickly turns to pleasure as she says, 'I want to feel your hard cock splitting me wide apart. ...Hurt me, hurt me.' This seems more like a male fantasy of his dominance (hardness, the power to split) and her submission (her pain *is* pleasure; her 'no' means 'yes'). As actress Georgina Spelvin wryly noted, 'It crosses my mind that taking it up the ass is much more erotic as a fantasy than when actually doing it. Miss Jones, however, gets into it.'[29] Spelvin is a little more direct about the extent to which a butt-plug scene did not fit *her* desires, calling it 'probably the most uncomfortable and humiliating thing I've ever done on film'.[30] Finally, there is the double penetration scene in which Miss Jones urges one man to 'put your prick further up my ass' and the other man to go 'further in my cunt' so that they will be 'filling me up completely... oh yes, all of it, all of you'. The fantasy of being completely filled up may be erotic, but the reality for Spelvin was enough physical discomfort that she had to *disconnect from* her body: 'It does take concentration – and a large degree of detachment. It's absolutely amazing what the human psyche will stand for if approached the right way.'[31] Rather than being about total fulfilment for her, this scene seems focused on how big the men's cocks are, on how deep they can penetrate. And then there is something else: 'Can you feel your cock against his?' Miss Jones asks her double penetrators. 'Can you feel your cocks together? Can you feel it in each other?' Does their homosexuality excite her, or is this such a male fantasy that it ends up excluding the woman entirely as the men get off on each other?

REAL SEX

Betty Blue (37°2 le matin) (1986)

Director: Jean-Jacques Beineix
Cast: Jean-Hugues Anglade (Zorg), Béatrice Dalle (Betty)

This film opens with one long-held shot that slowly zooms in on a naked couple engaged in intercourse. As the camera moves closer and closer, the man's thrusts become ever more deeply passionate until he and she reach orgasm at the moment of greatest intimacy. Though no penetration is shown, the shot is so graphically physical it gave rise to rumours that the actor and actress had actually had sex during this scene. And yet the shot also contains a distancing element: visible on the wall above the sexually intimate couple is a poster of the famously enigmatic *Mona Lisa*, suggesting that no matter how thoroughly this man 'knows' this woman in the carnal sense, she will always remain mysterious and unknowable. A friend shows the man (Zorg) a centrefold spread in a sex magazine and says that the photo looks like Zorg's lover (Betty). Then Zorg's boss, standing on a level below Betty, attempts to sneak a peek between her legs. In open defiance, she lifts up her clothes and blatantly displays her vulva to him, shouting 'Take a good look!' She enacts the role of sex object, fully exposing herself, while simultaneously saying that she is more than that, that she exceeds the limited part these men would have her play. The boss scolds her – 'You should be ashamed, bitch!' – for depriving him of the voyeuristic thrill of invading her innermost privacy against her will. Instead, she has made it clear that, while he may see her naked, she has not bared her soul.

Later, when Zorg slips off Betty's underwear, exposing her bush, and then begins to lick her, she pulls his head up to ask him whether he trusts her – whether their connection goes beyond the merely physical – before allowing him to continue. Cunnilingus is not sufficient; he must use his tongue to speak a deeper connection with her. In another scene, rather than wake Zorg up to have sex, Betty kisses his resting penis, calling it a 'warm, sleepy snail'. The physicality of this scene is not about desiring hardness or penetration but about loving the comfort of softness and allowing him the privacy of his own dreams. There are many scenes in which both Zorg and Betty are completely naked in front of each other as they move about the house doing their daily tasks. As one reviewer noted, 'For the first time in cinema, male nudity and female nudity are treated equally.'[32] The full-frontal nudity has a sexual charge but, pervasive and quotidian as it is, it also diffuses sensuality throughout and suggests the physical closeness and emotional comfort the two have in each other's presence, beyond the sexual sparks. It also reminds us of how much more these characters are than their bodies. We see them in their all, but do we really know them?

The Brown Bunny (2003)

Director: Vincent Gallo
Cast: Vincent Gallo (Bud), Chloë Sevigny (Daisy)

Bud and Daisy are in love. At a party, Bud looks through a cracked door and sees Daisy on her back in bed with two guys standing over her, one thrusting between her legs and the other in her mouth. At first Bud thinks the sex is consensual, but at some point he seems to realise that Daisy is being raped. However, claiming that he 'didn't know what to do', Bud does not intervene. He walks away and, when he later returns, is told that she choked on her own vomit and died. What is the reason for Bud's fatal uncertainty about what to do? Why doesn't he take decisive action and save Daisy from the assault? One possibility is that he never quite accepts the fact that it is rape. Maybe he was already insecure about Daisy's fidelity or nervous about dating such an overtly sexual woman, but a part of Bud seems to see his worst fears confirmed when he spies Daisy with those other men and to blame her for 'betraying' him.

Haunted by her memory, Bud imagines that Daisy appears to him in a hotel room where he has vaginal and oral sex with her. The fellatio begins in tenderness but becomes more violent as he moves from speaking endearments to extracting promises ('You won't suck anybody else's cock? Never? You promise me?') to making accusations ('Why did you suck that guy's cock? Why did you fuck those guys? ...Why did you let me see that?'). In close-up, we see him with one hand holding the base of his cock and the other hand on the back of her head as her mouth takes him in and out. The fellatio becomes a form of interrogation, with her bobbing head seeming to nod forced assent to his questions and with her groans sounding like 'uh-huhs'. At the climax of his excitement and his rage, he has her swallow his semen (we see her throat muscles working) and then pushes her away, calling her 'a fucking whore'. There is a reason why the real sex here has a pornographic explicitness. A part of Bud still believes that Daisy acted like a 'loose woman' in a 'porn scene' with those guys, and his imagined lovemaking with her is haunted by the memory of her having 'whored' around. In Bud's mind, the openly sexual way that Daisy behaves with him is proof of her whorish nature, and it provides an opportunity for him to punish her by taking her roughly. However, what we as viewers see is that Bud himself is essentially re-enacting what the two guys did to Daisy. He is raping her again – or perhaps it is his mind's way of realising his partial responsibility for the rape in that he stood and watched, as if he were viewing a porn scene, rather than intervening to stop it. Is Bud beginning to understand the extent to which he was complicit in sexual violence – and maybe even got off on it?

It's interesting to note that actress Chloë Sevigny (Daisy) was dropped by her talent agency for performing real sex in this film. Remarking on the fellatio scene, a source at the agency described it as 'one step above pornography, and not a very big one. William Morris now feels that her career is tainted and may never recover, especially after rumours began circulating about the even more graphic outtakes that didn't make it into the actual film.'[33] Ironically, Sevigny gets viewed and disdained as a porn actress for filming a scene that shows how her character is viewed and disdained for behaving like a porn actress – in the eyes of the male character, who is cruelly mistaken! For his part, Vincent Gallo – who directed and stars in the film as Bud – was accused of being narcissistic and exploitative for putting his cock up there on the screen and for having his lead actress suck it. Gallo's response is worth pondering: 'Pornography is the ability for somebody to have enhanced sexual pleasure or sexual fantasy free from responsibility, guilt, insecurity, consequence... What I've done is taken those icons of pornography and juxtaposed them against responsibility, insecurity, hate, greed, mourning... My character in The Brown Bunny cannot fill his mind with [healthy] sexuality. He cannot because he's filled with fear, grief, anger, and resentment. ...It's insight that I felt I had into pathological behaviour.'[34] And, regarding the close-ups of his penis, Gallo said, 'Do you think it's fun to show your cock in a film for ten billion to scrutinise for eternity? Do you think I get off on that?'[35]

9 Songs (2004)

Director: Michael Winterbottom
Cast: Kieran O'Brien (Matt), Margo Stilley (Lisa)

'Why do films *not* show sex?' asks director Michael Winterbottom. 'So many films are love stories, so why not show a love story through two people making love?'[36] For some viewers, though, this film's real sex resulted in a story without structure and in characters without depth: 'Winterbottom has picked up random moments in a relationship that is, finally, little more than the sum of sexual acts.'[37] But if this is the case, why did Winterbottom choreograph each sex scene so carefully? 'He really mapped out everything,' said actor Kieran O'Brien. 'He had specific ideas of how he wanted our bodies to move.'[38] The film's real sex does not mean that it has no story or character development but that the story and characters are developed *through the sex.*

In an early scene, Lisa wants Matt to give her some sexual attention. 'Fuck me,' she begs, 'please', and he has her say 'please' again and again. She undoes his belt and pulls on his erect cock, which is huge in her hand. When she puts her other hand near his mouth, he gives it a love bite, causing her to exclaim 'ow!' He backs her up against a desk and orders her to 'sit!' The first part of the scene emphasises her dependency and need next to his superior size and dominance. But at this point he kneels before her, kissing her breasts and tonguing her sex as she sits above him on the desk, the camera showing her pleasure-filled face with bright sun shining on it. She then bids him to rise and 'fuck me'. Unlike before, she is clearly in command this time, directing him to 'do it faster' and eventually to 'come inside me'.

In a later scene, Matt and Lisa go to a sex club where she gets excited when a female stripper does a lap dance on her. Views of Lisa kissing the dancer's breasts are cross-cut with shots of Lisa at home touching her own breasts and using a vibrator between her legs. After watching Lisa masturbate to orgasm in bed by herself, Matt turns away, just as he also walks out of the strip club. Seeing Lisa take pleasure on her own or with another woman, Matt feels excluded, perhaps fearing that he is inadequate. But Lisa might find fulfilment in him while also wanting to experience auto-eroticism and lesbianism. Is the man insufficient just because the woman enjoys her own sex?

The Raspberry Reich (2004)

Director: Bruce LaBruce
Cast: Susanne Sachsse (Gudrun), Daniel Bätscher (her boyfriend Holger)

Gudrun, the leader of an ultra-leftist gang, believes that political revolution must include sexual revolution. Susanne Sachsse, who plays Gudrun, 'felt as an actress that it was important for her to "go the distance" and perform in a sexually explicit scene in the movie', to 'make it sexually real as a reinforcement of the ideals of sexual liberation being espoused by the movie', according to director Bruce LaBruce.[39] Thus the sex we see Gudrun engage in with her boyfriend is real, involving graphic penetration. Yet this commitment to sexual liberation is also satirised as programmatic and hyperbolic, for Gudrun insists on avoiding the missionary position on the bourgeois bed in order to perform all other sex acts serially in every room. She particularly likes sex up against a wall while pumping her fist and shouting slogans such as 'Out of the bedrooms! On to the streets!' Ironically, Gudrun often seems more committed to the idea or image of sexual revolution than to the reality; her by-the-book sexual programme seems the opposite of free love. It should be noted, though, that an older married couple – who see Gudrun having sex in the elevator and critique it as being for show ('This is outrageous and obscene! What do you think you're trying to prove?') – are themselves inspired enough by the sight to make love as soon as they return to their apartment.

To prove their commitment to the cause, Gudrun wants all the straight men around her to 'throw off the shackles of heterosexual monogamy' and engage in gay sex. She plans to videotape a same-sex scene involving a young man they have kidnapped and to show it to his father, pushing it right into the face of 'heterosexual conformity'. This video is like the very film we are watching, which pushes homo sex into the faces of straight audiences, and hetero sex into the faces of gay audiences. As LaBruce says, 'Most heterosexual men have fixed themselves in a rigid role which doesn't even allow the possibility of bi- or homo-sexual impulses... Homosexual men have likewise fixed themselves in a gay identity which doesn't allow the possibility of sex with females.'[40] 'But I can't just automatically go gay all of a sudden,' protests one of Gudrun's men incredulously, and indeed the idea does seem ridiculous; yet when a friend fellates him, suggesting that he watch straight porn during the act, this man finds that he *can* slide into a different sexuality. When Gudrun's boyfriend tells her he thought they were engaged, she replies that 'The revolution is my boyfriend!' Is this free love or a different kind of repression – of her own desires squelched by political posturing? After watching her fiancé fellate another man, Gudrun swings to the opposite extreme at the end of the film, marrying her boyfriend and having a child together. Has she joined the ranks of the conformist bourgeoisie, or is marriage now the ultimate revolution because, unlike her pre-scripted pronouncements of free love, getting married is an act of her own radical will?

All About Anna (2005)

Director: Jessica Nilsson
Cast: Gry Bay (Anna), Mark Stevens (Johan), Ovidie (Sophie)

All About Anna was a troubled production. The film was originally to be made in accord with the 'Puzzy Power Manifesto' whereby it would 'present sensuality (or sexually explicit material, if you like) in a way that appeals to women'.[41] However, if producer Nicolas Barbano is to be believed, the director (Jessica Nilsson) decided that 'she didn't really want to show any hardcore in the film because she thought genitals were disgusting'.[42] Similarly, according to actor Mark Stevens, the lead actress (Gry Bay) 'didn't really want to show anything' and 'that's why you'll never see an actual penetration shot or any of her actual genitalia'.[43] Lest we assume that these complaints – here made by two men – are merely what we would expect from a male audience 'deprived' of hardcore, it's worth noting that another actress in the film, feminist porn star Ovidie, also said that 'there's one thing that frustrates me: ...I have not seen – not even once – Gry's pussy in this movie. ...It's true we see the actor's cock... but we don't see the woman's genitals. ...I like seeing the woman's genitals. I think it's beautiful.'[44]

The finished film is a fascinating composite of competing interests. By all accounts, mainstream actors did engage in real sex for this film and there are shots of erections, ejaculations, and oral penetrations. However, these latter are inserts of a body double's mouth shot separately by the producer because Gry Bay refused to do them. There are no vaginal close-up or penetration shots, and Bay can sometimes be seen using her hands to cover her vulva and even her breasts. The film thus oscillates between hardcore and soft, uncertain what to show despite its 'Puzzy Power Manifesto'. It is intended as a film 'made by women, for women',[45] but what do women want? As Ovidie notes, 'It's so difficult to know what each woman wants to see, doesn't want to see' or 'what [women will] admit that they like to watch'[46] – especially in a society where female exposure on film tends to be associated with more degrading forms of pornography made by and for men. One difference between All About Anna and traditional porn is that, instead of fragmented editing and isolated 'meat shots', the camera tends to move back and forth between upper and lower bodies, between kissing faces and thrusting hips. This would seem to fit with the Manifesto's call to give sex a face, 'to integrate explicit sex as part of the storytelling and character development'.[47] Or it could be the result of the director's not wanting to face sex: 'She was very disturbed by images of naked people and especially naked people having sex. So she made it this style where the camera sort of by accident happened to shoot something that was perhaps pornographic.'[48] Or it could be both.

Lie with Me (2005)

Director: Clément Virgo
Cast: Lauren Lee Smith (Leila), Eric Balfour (David)

'Are our real emotions in words or in our physicality?' asks director Clément Virgo.[49] To understand the relationship between the characters of Leila and David, we have to read their 'gestures' and 'body language'.[50] When they first meet at a party, David watches Leila dancing sexily with two other men. She leads one of these guys outside where she uses fellatio to get him hard and then rides him. All the while, she sees that David is watching her from across the way, and Leila, too, looks on as David's girlfriend gives him head and then climbs on top of him. Excitement is fuelled by voyeurism and exhibitionism, by being tantalised and made jealous. During this mutual gazing, there is the sense that each really wants to be with the other, that the guy's and the girlfriend's bodies are merely intermediaries and impediments to Leila and David's coming together, that their sex acts form mirror images because they want them to be one and the same. Thus, troilism – watching one's partner have sex with another – both fuels desire and frustrates its true fulfilment.

Later, David chases Leila into a park where there is a kiddie playground. As he sits inside a big plastic tube, she squats at its entrance, first holding her dress down demurely and coyly, then lifting it to reveal her pantied crotch. While sexually charged (the self-exposure, the phallic tube), this scene also has a sense of childhood innocence, as if the two were kids playfully discovering their sexuality in a game of 'I'll show you mine if you show me yours'. Indeed, Leila then takes down one side of her halter top to expose a breast, and David begins to knead his crotch with his hand. However, when Leila herself begins to masturbate with her hand down her panties, David stops and runs away like a frightened boy. Virgo notes that 'there's a lot of judgement' of 'female sexuality': 'a lot of guys are still kind of shocked that women want it or desire it as much as they do'.[51]

In another scene, after watching Leila enjoy herself dancing while sandwiched between two other guys, David calls her a 'slut' and asks her, 'Have you ever had one man's dick in your ass and his friend's cock in your mouth?' When she tries to fellate him, David has her bend over so that he can take her anally, causing her pain. David may be excited by the image of her with other men, but he is also violently jealous. By forcing himself on her anally, he puts himself in place of the other man's body and reclaims his own 'rightful possession' of her. He also punishes her for thinking that she has a right to her own desire for someone other – or something more – than him. Her desire is too much for him because he fears he won't be enough to satisfy it. When David drops his trousers after not letting Leila take him in her mouth, the camera shows his flaccid penis. Her desire turns him off when he doesn't feel equal to it. It is only the ensuing act of anal domination that gets him hard.

Enter the Void (2009)

Director: Gaspar Noé
Cast: Nathaniel Brown (Oscar), Paz de la Huerta (Linda), Cyril Roy (Alex), Masato Tanno (Mario)

Director Gaspar Noé has said, 'I saw my parents making love when I was a child. Obviously, I was very shocked. One always idealises one's parents as higher spiritual beings, whereas they too are animals, like me, like everybody.'[52] In *Enter the Void*, young Oscar opens a door to discover his father's naked body thrusting into his mother's on their bed. Afterwards, Oscar asks his mother, 'Do you love Daddy more than you love me?' Then both his parents are killed in a car accident. For Oscar, sex has come to represent exclusion and death. First there is a kind of exile from the womb: when his father's body is in his mother's, Oscar's cannot be. Then there is the mortality of the flesh: because his mother has a body, she can die – as Oscar will, too.

After he is shot dead by police during a drug raid, Oscar's spirit floats above the world, looking down as his sister Linda does a pole dance in a nightclub. Being his sister, Linda naturally 'resembles his mother', and Oscar 'makes sort of a transference from his mother onto his sister'.[53] As Linda twirls around the pole and writhes up and down its length, the camera – taking Oscar's perspective from above, representing his spirit looking down on her – turns round and round as if dancing with her, and rises and plunges, too, as if he were the pole in motion. Later, Oscar's hovering spirit watches as Linda takes out her boss Mario's hard cock so that he can put it in her. As Mario is thrusting, Oscar floats through the back of Mario's head so that he can see Linda's pleasure-filled face but then floats back out. Once again, sex seems to exclude him: Mario's body, like the pole, is there where Oscar's is not. Oscar cannot connect love and flesh. The loving, disembodied Oscar seems forever separate from the world of flesh and fucking;

he is tantalised by it but also seems to fear its association with mortality. Interestingly, Linda and Mario's coupling prevents her from taking a phone call about Oscar's death. It's almost as though he were killed by their having sex; their physical link cuts his loving tie with his sister and with life itself.

In a later scene, though, as the Oscar-camera floats from room to room above couples having sex in a Love Hotel, bright light emanates from the points of contact between their bodies: mouth and penis, mouth and vagina, penis and vagina. The encounters are corporeal – the sex is real – but there is also an ethereal quality, as though Oscar were seeking a way through the physical to the spiritual, a way to see the two as continuous rather than separate or opposed. In one of the rooms, Oscar floats down through the back of his best friend Alex's head to see Linda's face, with the camera moving in and out on her as Alex is thrusting. Linda then looks over to see the young Oscar standing in the doorway, watching. What Oscar sees is love and not just pleasure on his sister's face, for she is enamoured of Alex (whereas Mario was just 'a good fuck'). 'Come, come inside me,' Linda says, and the Oscar-camera – looking out from within Linda's vagina – sees Alex's penis thrust and ejaculate inside her. Noé notes that 'the image of the penis coming at the camera at the end was not meant to be funny. ...I thought it would be epic or mythological or dramatic. ...If you saw it in your own dreams, you would not laugh.'[54] This is Oscar's dream of being reunited with his sister and his mother. Lowly body and higher spirit – real sex and ideal love – can be reconciled. At this point, Oscar flashes back to the moment his mother gave birth to him, or he flashes forward to his reincarnation and rebirth as his sister's baby. Either way, Oscar finds that sex doesn't kill him; it brings him back to life.

Now & Later (2009)

Director: Philippe Diaz
Cast: James Wortham (Bill), Shari Solanis (Angela), Adrian Quinonez (her lover Diego)

Now & Later is an indie film with graphic sex. Director Philippe Diaz has said he wanted to show that 'sex and all its components (erection, ejaculation, masturbation, as well as any and all forms of sexual pleasures)' are 'as natural as eating food, listening to music or simply enjoying life'.[55] For bourgeois banker Bill, sex was always something to be ashamed and afraid of – even when sanctified by marriage and directed towards procreation. But Angela, an illegal immigrant who shelters Bill after his greed gets him into trouble with the law, nurtures in him a new understanding of the body. After a meal, she has him close his eyes and just feel while she fellates him, establishing a sensual continuity between the two kinds of 'eating'. She puts on music, too, so that aural and oral combine to overcome visual shame. In another scene, she coaxes him to display his erection; she openly masturbates him; and she has mirrors so that he can see himself thrusting during sex with her. 'Did you enjoy watching yourself?' she asks, getting beyond guilt and restoring sight to the list of erotic senses. It's important that we as viewers also see Bill's erection, for the film wants *us* – along with the character – to overcome fear and shame in order to take visual pleasure. At the same time, Bill's hard-on is never isolated in close-up as it would be in porn films. It is always seen with the rest of his body in the frame, and the emphasis is on his face. In this way, the sex organ is represented as continuous with the body as a whole and with the humanity of the person who is feeling pleasure.

And yet, when Angela invites Bill to a threesome in bed and places his hand around the erection of her male lover, Bill says 'I can't' and leaves the bed. Is Bill still prevented by guilt from experiencing certain kinds of pleasure, even though he had earlier confessed a secret desire to hold another man's cock and feel him come?[56] Or does Bill resist because his true love is Angela and he doesn't want to make love to, or share her with, anyone else? A sexual existentialist, Angela has enabled Bill to find sensual enjoyment in the moment, to live for 'now', but is it hopelessly bourgeois of him to think that there might be a 'later', that through sex they might form a lasting and exclusive bond? If he can't just give himself over to endlessly varied sensual pleasure because it matters to him whose body he is holding and who gives rise to his enjoyment, does that make him prudish and possessive? It is a sign of this film's strength that it prompts such questions.

SCIENCE FICTION

The Man Who Fell to Earth (1976)

Director: Nicolas Roeg
Cast: David Bowie (the alien), Candy Clark (Mary-Lou/alien wife)

With his orange hair, androgynous look and bisexuality, rock star David Bowie may already seem like an alien from another planet to some people – particularly in his Ziggy Stardust 'space invader' persona. In this film, he plays an alien who comes to Earth and, taking on the outward appearance of a man, establishes an emotional connection with a woman (Mary-Lou). The trouble occurs when the two try to make love. When the alien removes his human contact lenses, he reveals yellow eyes that look like a cat's or a demon's to her. The difference between them seems too great, as if in being with him she would be having sex with an animal or a devil. Nevertheless, she attempts to make physical contact with him. As he lies naked in bed, she runs her hand over his body but all she feels is absence: he has no hair on his chest or anywhere else and is devoid of male genitalia. However, there is a viscous white substance, possibly emitted by his nipples, which his hand rubs on her breasts, causing her to scream and run away. Is she frightened by difference or by too much *sameness*? With breasts instead of balls, with a sexuality of mutual touch rather than aggressive thrusting, the alien would seem to be more 'feminine' than manly. Is it the possibility of a 'lesbian' encounter that scares her?

Or is she afraid of sex as something at once similar and different, something mysterious and indefinable? It's not clear what the white substance is (milk? semen?) or whether it comes from his nipples, his groin or some other site on his body. Perhaps the alien is polymorphously perverse and the substance comes from his entire epidermis. Rather than having discrete erogenous zones, his whole body – from his bald head down to his hairless chest and lower extremities – may be a sex organ, his entire length like a penis or breast. In his memories of lovemaking back on his home planet, the alien recalls that he and his wife would smear the white substance on each other's bodies until they were covered head to toe in it, coming together in its sticky flow. But this kind of gender fluidity is too much for Mary-Lou; it is felt as too great a threat to the conventional masculine and feminine boundaries she is used to on Earth. Ironically, the same actress plays both the human Mary-Lou and the alien wife, lending pathos to the fact that Mary-Lou was unable to find herself in the other, to get beyond her limitations and find fulfilment in different forms of sexuality.

Café Flesh (1982)

Director: Rinse Dream (Stephen Sayadian)
Cast: Michelle Bauer (Lana), Paul McGibboney (Nick), Andy Nichols (the emcee)

Café Flesh is a unique combination of hardcore porn and post-apocalyptic science fiction – and it's also a musical! The film is set in a dystopian future where 99% of the people are Sex Negatives who can no longer express love physically without falling ill. These people go to nightclubs where the remaining 1%, the Positives, are forced to perform sexual acts for the voyeuristic Negatives. Two of the audience members, Lana and Nick, are typical: they're in love but they can't have sex. This couple watches as stage performers have sex but without love. This dystopian separation between love and sex can be taken as a commentary on viewers of hardcore porn who watch, hoping that it will improve their love life, but finding only emotionless sex. As the club's emcee says with dark sarcasm, 'Kind of exciting, huh? Hey, not too pathetic that the biggest night of your life is watching some strange palooka get his hog washed by some bimbo you don't even know?' The film might also be saying that viewers' addiction to porn may make it impossible for them to do or enjoy the real thing, as a craving for mere sensation replaces the desire for true intimacy. In one on-stage sex act, a man in a rat mask uses his snout to sniff out the female sex. Theirs is a dehumanised, anonymous encounter between animals, where the sense of smell is isolated from all the other senses and feelings that normally combine to make up a human being. In another act, a Texas tycoon in a pencil mask checks a stock chart and then plunges in and out of a woman, while oil derricks pump in the background. Here porn reduces the body to a machine for making money or for proving potency.

However, some of the staged scenes demonstrate a need to link this dehumanised humping back to the head and the heart. There is a man with his head in a box who tries to extend his tongue beyond its confines to lick the woman seated on top. If they wanted it badly enough, perhaps the Negatives could reconnect love to sex, moving beyond voyeurism to enactment. As the emcee says, 'The skull in the cage knows that the real bars are always behind the eyes.' Another scene about the desire to reconnect shows a woman trapped in a phone booth while, on the other side of the glass, another woman has sex with a man wearing a telephone mask. 'Watch,' the emcee has said. 'Our humble spectacle might just be able to make you almost *feel*.' 'Be positive,' he tells Lana, as if watching the porn scenes could help her become a Sex Positive again, exciting her body so that she can reunite it with her mind. Perhaps her nausea at the thought of having sex isn't due to atomic fallout but is instead a mental block, a puritanical disgust at her own body or a fear of a physical encounter with another's flesh. In the end, the staged sex acts inspire Lana to get back in touch with her body through masturbation. Then, after watching a formerly Sex-Negative virgin enjoy sex, Lana takes that woman's place and does the act herself with a porn stud. Unfortunately, Nick – her true paramour – is unable to get beyond his sex negativity, so Lana isn't really able to make love with the man she loves. Has she in fact brought fucking and feeling together, or did she just satisfy her lust for the porn stud's '10-inch' cock?

Splice (2009)

Director: Vincenzo Natali
Cast: Sarah Polley (Elsa), Delphine Chanéac (Dren), Adrien Brody (Clive)

Biotechnologist Elsa splices some of her own human DNA into that of several animals. The resulting creature, Dren, has the head and breasts of a woman combined with a bird's wings, an amphibian's lungs, a kangaroo's legs and a stingray's tail. Elsa's partner in research and love, Clive, feels a strange attraction to Dren. On the one hand, he seems to be excited by her wild animal desire – the movie's metaphor for a strong female sexuality. On the other hand, such assertiveness on the part of the opposite sex disturbs and frightens him, for it exceeds the role that woman is expected to play in the conventional mating ritual with man, which is flirtatious but compliant, a little forward but ultimately passive in relation to *his* dominance. Clive is already upset by how dominant Elsa is in her relationship with him and so he tries to become top man again with Dren, Elsa's DNA-sharing substitute.

Thus, when Clive and Dren dance together and she tries to take the lead, he keeps telling her to 'back up' because 'the man leads'. Later, she throws herself at him, wrapping her bird wings around his body and kissing him, but he pushes her away, feeling overwhelmed and trapped because *she* made the advances. Just before this, she stood behind him with her wings outstretched, which made it look as though her wings were on his body. In a sense, this is what he seems to want from coupling with her: by taming her wildness, he hopes to acquire her animal power. It doesn't seem to occur to him that they could both be wild together; instead, he must master her savagery to prove that he is more primally powerful. When Dren backs Clive up against a wall and uses her tail to grip a support so that she can wrap one leg around him in a passionate embrace, he pushes her down onto the floor to penetrate her while she lies on her back. She, however, rolls over on top to ride him, with her wings outspread and her face in ecstasy, showing that she takes her own proud pleasure and is more than just the means to his. He then grabs her head and rolls her over so that he's on top, thrusting into her in the missionary position, trying to 'tame the shrew'.

But she orgasms, and the movie shows how he feels her female pleasure to be a threat to him by having her tail rise up as she comes, its needle-stinger protracting as it approaches the back of his head. An actively desiring female, one who takes her own pleasure, is thus not only a wild animal but a phallic menace threatening to 'rape' the man. The movie figures this by having Dren actually change sex from female to male like a serial hermaphrodite. Later, when Clive tries to assert his superior manhood by piercing Dren with a pole, Dren kills Clive with a needle-stab to the heart – a fitting end for a man who chose dominance over love.

EROTIC THEMES

ADDICTION

Shame (2011)

Director: Steve McQueen
Cast: Michael Fassbender (Brandon), Carey Mulligan (Sissy)

Brandon is a New York City yuppie who is outwardly happy and successful but secretly driven to feed his lust in an endless round of sex, shame and more sex to forget the shame. As director Steve McQueen has said, 'Brandon is living in Manhattan in this metropolis of excess and Western freedom. He has a great job, he's attractive, he has money. Within those possibilities, he creates a prison for himself through his activities with sex. ...A prison with no bars. Maybe it's too much freedom.'[57] Porn – the 'filthy' kind with 'hos, sluts, anal, double anal' – is readily available on his home and office computers, and Brandon is a chronic masturbator, jerking off in his apartment shower, his office toilet and anywhere else he can find to do it. He has compulsive intercourse with pick-ups and prostitutes, voraciously consuming each one before moving on to the next.

One day, though, his sister Sissy comes to stay with him and, when he overhears her having sex with his married boss in the next room, Brandon is horribly reminded of a trauma from their past, perhaps a time when he heard their father molesting her.

After the boss leaves, Sissy enters Brandon's room and gets into bed with him – maybe as she, prematurely sexualised, had done when they were children – prompting him to order her to 'get the fuck out!' If there was incestuous abuse – a precocious and improper intimacy in their family, this could account for the barrier Brandon has erected to separate flesh from feeling. He can have sex but it must be emotionless and anonymous, like the encounter he witnesses of a man screwing a woman from behind while she is pressed up against the glass of a hotel window. What should be a private act is deprived of intimacy and made public in front of his fascinated gaze, like his earlier traumatic hearing, or witnessing, of incestuous violation.

Yet, when Sissy catches him masturbating and when she discovers all the porn on his computer (with their obscene images reflected on her face), Brandon resolves to overcome his sex addiction for her sake, realising that his behaviour only perpetuates the sexual wound inflicted on her and himself when they were young. He goes on a real date with a woman from work, but when removing his clothes means letting his emotional guard down, too, he finds himself unable to get an erection. Later, taking a woman doggy-style up against a window, he has no trouble getting hard, for this – bestial and essentially predatory – is what sex has been to him, following on the pattern set for him long ago by his abusive father. But Brandon does not give up trying. He makes lewd advances to a woman in front of her boyfriend in an attempt to provoke an outside authority to step in and stop his predation. He presses a gay man into giving him head – something that, to Brandon, is apparently repugnant. (Was he forced to do this as a child?) He even screws two women in the same bed as if to thoroughly sate himself on female flesh. In the end, we see Brandon eyeing a woman on a subway train just as he was doing at the film's beginning. Will he follow and fuck her, or remember his sister and resist the urge?

BISEXUALITY

Savage Nights (Les nuits fauves) (1992)

Director: Cyril Collard
Cast: Cyril Collard (Jean), Carlos López (Samy), Romane Bohringer (Laura)

On his 'savage nights', Jean has sex with multiple male partners in public cruising grounds. He also seduces an ostensibly straight rugby player, Samy, whose body turns him on. But then Jean meets Laura, a practically virginal teen with whom he engages in a romantic flirtation. The two make love but he doesn't come, because for him passion is linked to homosexuality. Jean thus lives a life divided between hetero romance and same-sex passion: 'I loved Laura, I loved Samy, loved the vices of my savage nights. Was I born so completely divided?'[58]

Perhaps owing to internalised homophobia, Jean does see sex with men as a 'vice' and, when he becomes infected with AIDS, the images of all those he has been with blur and meld into that of the virus. By contrast, Jean has unprotected sex with Laura because he believes that his virtuous love for her will cleanse him of his sins and prevent her from contracting the disease. However, as he soon realises, 'I was a coward. I thought I was coming to Laura washed of the stains from my nights, while silently exposing her to the corruption of my blood. I was shooting my virus into her.'[59] When Jean does tell her that he is HIV-positive and insists that they use a condom, he takes the first step towards integrating sex and romance, for, if he really loves her, he cannot deny her the truth about his body, which unavoidably affects hers as well.

Jean's sexual experiences with others have contributed to his skill as a lover: 'Laura doesn't know the most sordid details of the depths my nights bring me to, but I know she senses those savage nights are the reason I can make her come like nobody else, because they're a part of me.'[60] Yet, despite having sex with Laura in one of his public cruising spots, Jean is unable to recapture with her the passion of his all-male encounters. For this reason, he continues to have casual sex with others, including the macho Samy. Jean seems to want Laura to have smaller breasts and to cut her hair, and she accuses Jean of imagining Samy while making love to her. But when Samy himself softens, beginning to drink herbal tea and declaring his love for Jean, Jean leaves him for more purely physical encounters with other men. The end of the film finds Jean looking (desirously?) at some young men while telling Laura (on the phone) that he loves her. Jean seems happy, as though he has somehow healed – or accepted – the split in his psyche, but has he? And, if so, how?

Kinsey (2004)

Director: Bill Condon
Cast: Liam Neeson (Kinsey), Peter Sarsgaard (Martin), Laura Linney (Mac)

Kinsey is a zoologist who begins researching and teaching courses in *human* sexuality. In this, he is opposed by Professor Thurman, who promotes abstinence using scare-tactic sex-ed films detailing the ravages of venereal disease. If sexually tempting thoughts keep him awake, Thurman tells his students, 'I like to close my eyes and think of all the Johns I know. Well, not only Johns, sometimes Peters.' The class laughs that Thurman could be so oblivious to his own *double entendres*, but these may also be slips of the tongue signifying repressed desires, particularly given that Thurman is played by actor Tim Curry, who starred as one of film history's most famous bisexuals in *The Rocky Horror Picture Show* (1975).

The ostensibly hetero Kinsey has also been tempted. When he was an Eagle Scout and when a boy his junior sought his help regarding lustful thoughts, Kinsey had the two of them pray rather than masturbate together. As a professor, Kinsey is quick to adopt an adoring student named Martin as his assistant. As Kinsey reads to his class from a list of sex questions – 'Is it unusual for my boyfriend to touch my anus?' – the film cuts to a shot of Martin standing behind Kinsey in a hint of gay desires still only in the back of his mind. In a later scene, the two men are half-naked as Kinsey stands behind Martin to show him that he's been 'using the wrong muscle group' while digging in the garden. This moment of Adam and Steve in Eden is interrupted by the arrival of Kinsey's wife, Mac, who brings with her a shaming gaze, making the men feel awkward about their nudity and closeness. Still later, after interviewing men in a gay bar, Kinsey and Martin share a hotel room. Martin emerges naked from the shower and only very gradually dons pyjamas. 'I took maybe a little bit too long putting on my clothes,' says actor Peter Sarsgaard. 'I wanted to throw it out there to his character, like if you think I'm doing something, then I'm doing something; if you don't think I'm doing something, I'm totally not doing something – I'm putting on my clothes and going to bed.'[61] Martin's seduction involves an appeal to Kinsey's unconscious, asking whether he wants to acknowledge and act on his repressed homoerotic desires. In addition, the guilt-ridden Kinsey may be attracted to Martin because the younger man shows an uninhibited acceptance of his own body. Director Bill Condon has remarked upon actor Sarsgaard's 'incredible comfort with his own body and being naked. ...I don't think I've met anybody who's as comfortable in his own skin, just a great person to be around, the most open person.'[62]

The fact that Kinsey has sex with Martin that night does not establish Kinsey as a 'closeted homosexual' who finally 'comes out' as definitively 'gay'. In addition to sleeping with Martin (who has feminine traits), Kinsey continues to make love with his wife, Mac (who has masculine attributes), and even engages in a threesome with Martin and a woman. In this film, the point of the 'Kinsey scale' – where 0 is exclusively hetero and 6 is exclusively homo – is that the vast majority of people are somewhere in the middle, sliding along a bisexual continuum of both/and rather than either/or. As Condon has said, 'Kinsey's basic idea... is that everyone's sexuality is unique. ...for him there's no freedom in defining yourself by your sexual acts'.[63]

DISABILITY

The Waterdance (1992)

Directors: Neal Jimenez, Michael Steinberg
Cast: Eric Stoltz (Joel), Helen Hunt (Anna)

After breaking his neck in a hiking accident, Joel is permanently paralysed from the waist down. With other paraplegics at the rehabilitation centre, he attends a sex therapy lecture where they are told that, while they can get an erection, it's not likely to feel the same and that achieving orgasm is very rare. Feeling unmanned, the men turn their rage on each other. 'You're a little prick,' one of them says to Joel, taunting him about the imminent loss of his girlfriend: 'How long do you think it's gonna take before that pretty little girl of yours leaves you for somebody who can tune her engine?' Thinking of sexuality in the most conventionally masculine terms (of using a wrench on a car), the men fear that they lack the tool to do the job.

Co-director Neal Jimenez, himself a paraplegic, described the characters as 'men having to redefine their manhood when their physical being is entirely changed'.[64] When his girlfriend Anna kisses his hand and strokes his arm as he is lying in the hospital bed, Joel initially baulks. The passive position he is in feels unmanly (he is unused to her making the advances) and he considers himself ill-equipped to respond (his arm seems like a poor substitute for the organ that used to have more feeling).

However, her persistence eventually leads him to take action by holding her face between his hands to passionately kiss her and then by reaching into her panties to masturbate her. This scene marks the first time in a mainstream film that a man has masturbated a woman to orgasm. It would seem that Hollywood, along with Joel, is discovering that there are equally valid forms of male sexual expression besides thrusting during intercourse. Later, in a hotel bed, as Anna lies on top of him, Joel has her sit up so that he can see her breasts: 'I want to look at you.' 'The movie is erotic because, in Joel's new body, he has to deal with the visual rather than the tactile,' says Jimenez.[65] For Joel, sight gains in importance as a mode of sexual response as the feeling in his penis lessens. The movie does not sentimentalise Joel's changed bodily experience. He rages at the loss of what he once had: 'My girlfriend, she touches me now and I don't feel a thing. I feel nothing. ...I hate her for walking, for feeling.' However, as Jimenez notes regarding the depiction of sexuality in the film, 'We deal as much with possibility as we do with loss.'[66]

Elegy (2008)

Director: Isabel Coixet
Cast: Ben Kingsley (David), Penélope Cruz (Consuela), Dennis Hopper (George)

David is a divorced professor who indulges in a series of affairs with students. He seduces one such student, Consuela, by saying that she resembles the woman in Goya's painting of *The Nude Maja*. As she lies beneath him in bed, her body displayed like Maja's, he tells her, 'You have the most beautiful breasts I've ever seen. ...And you have a beautiful face I can't stop looking at. You're a work of art.' Does he praise her beauty just to get her naked, or is he finally discovering a woman's face through her flesh? Art was supposed to be his alibi for sex. As his philandering friend George says, 'Bifurcate your requirements: ...look at all the Goyas that you want, but keep the sex part just for sex.' David has always had a thing for breasts; women with beautiful ones became the instant object of his lust. (In fact, David once imagined himself transformed into a giant female breast.)[67] But, in Consuela, David suddenly finds himself attracted to a beauty that is more than skin deep. Rather than tasting her flesh and then moving on to other mammalian treats, he misses her when they're apart and jealously imagines her in the arms of rival men: 'I knew it's only a matter of time before a young man found her and took her away. I knew because I was once that young man who'd have done it.' It is as though the ageing David splits into two selves, one with the maturity to appreciate Consuela's whole being, and the other – his former self – just lusting after her breasts. But now that David is nearing emotional maturity, he fears that his physical body is no longer attractive to a young woman like Consuela. The relationship falters because he will not let himself be seen in public with her, so jealous is he of others' youth and fearful of their eyes upon him, condemning him as too old for her. Age becomes his sexual disability.

Then Consuela is diagnosed with breast cancer and she asks David to photograph her before the surgery, telling him that 'I never had a boyfriend who loved my body as much as you did.' With this request, Consuela separates David from her other, more superficial lovers. Like them, David desired her for her flesh, but his was a love so deep it encompassed her whole being. She needs this love now, for her fear is that, when a part of her is gone, he will no longer be able to see her whole: 'Will you still want to fuck me if I lose my breast? Will you be up for that?' What if these body parts – the beautiful breast and the youthful erection so vitally important to their lovemaking – were gone? Can love survive the ravages of disease and the decay of old age? David does come to Consuela's bedside following the mastectomy. It could be argued that the film flinches in not showing what her body now looks like, when it did show her breasts before. However, couldn't it also be said that the missing part is of much less significance than what we do see, which is her face?

GAY

Sebastiane (1976)

Directors: Derek Jarman, Paul Humfress
Cast: Neil Kennedy (Max), Ken Hicks (Adrian), Janusz Romanov (Anthony), Leonardo Treviglio (Sebastian), Barney James (Severus)

AD 303. A group of Roman soldiers is encamped at an isolated outpost far from women and 'civilisation'. Max taunts some of the other men for their homosexual behaviour: 'I don't know why you fancy boys so much. ...They're okay for a quick one, but I can't wait for Rome and a real woman.' However, Max's mockery is so pervasive and insistent that it seems to convey his own desires. As the troops awake, Max grabs in jest(?) at their morning erections, and he dons a dildo which he pretends(?) to stick in their mouths and rear ends. Max calls Adrian 'Adriana' and tells Anthony to 'screw him – that's what you want', but it would seem that that's what Max himself really wants. The bulbous fake nose that Max wears, like the dildo, sword and spear he also has at various times, suggests that he is constantly excited by the men around him – or trying to defend himself against his own same-sex desires. 'Dancing girl!' is how Max jeers at one soldier. 'Whore! Why don't you put on a dress?' But when Max mimics him by making up his own face, doing a lascivious dance and then kissing and fondling the men, the mockery would seem to go pretty far, turning into a true imitation. At least consciously, though, Max despises effeminacy and thinks of himself as a real man and a hardened soldier, and that hardness – the verbal aggression and the violence with phallic weapons – seems to be the only way he can convey his homosexual impulses.

If the military repression of Max's same-sex desires turns them towards sadism, then religious repression channels Sebastian's homosexuality into masochism. A recent convert to Christianity, the former soldier Sebastian now refuses to fight, just as he refuses to have anything to do with his captain Severus's aggressive sexual advances: 'Poor Severus! You think your drunken lust compares to the love of gods? ...You've never had me and you never will!' But, admirable though it may seem at first, Sebastian's position against violence goes beyond pacifism to become an extreme passivity, a voluptuous masochism. When Severus has him whipped, burned with a candle and bound spread-eagled and exposed to the sun, Sebastian worships his tormentor, finding ecstasy in the pain: 'His body is golden, like molten gold. ...He is as beautiful as the sun. ...His beauty is enhanced by his anger. It is his anger which is divine. His punishments are like Christ's promise.' In the end, Severus has the soldiers tie Sebastian to a stake and shoot arrows into his naked body. Because of repression, this violent penetration is the only way they can express their love for him. And Sebastian finds glory in his suffering, with his body arched and his head thrown back in ecstasy. Repression means that the only kind of sensual enjoyment he can allow himself is one that comes through pain. The film climaxes in sado-masochism.

Beautiful Thing (1996)

Director: Hettie Macdonald
Cast: Glen Berry (Jamie), Scott Neal (Ste)

In *Beautiful Thing*, Jonathan Harvey 'wanted to write a working class gay love story with a happy ending'.[68] The film's tagline is 'an urban fairytale', delicately balanced as it is between the real (poverty, violence, homophobia) and the ideal (young romance).

While living in a South London housing project, Jamie and Ste are two teenage boys who fall in love. In one scene, Jamie sucks on an iced lollipop while watching Ste play football. A child's innocent enjoyment here shades almost imperceptibly into erotic excitement, taste into sight as Jamie begins to take in the pleasure of athletic bodies as well as ice-cream treats. Later, he catches a glimpse of Ste's bare ass as the boy is changing, while also noticing the livid bruises on his back where he was beaten by his alcoholic father. Lust turns quickly to sympathy or, rather, the two commingle as Jamie's feelings *for* Ste's body lead him to feel *with* the other boy, to sense pain in the body that Jamie would like to pleasure.

When Ste finds refuge from his father by staying in the flat where Jamie lives with his mother, cramped quarters mean that the two boys must sleep 'top to tail' in the same bed. This phrase, repeated several times in the film, gradually changes its meaning from a poverty-induced proximity to something more sexually suggestive, as if to hint at 69ing. Initially, though, the boys are awkward and tentative together in bed. As Ste lies on his stomach, Jamie squirts and rubs peppermint foot lotion onto his back to soothe his wounds. Maternal care (the lotion is Jamie's mum's) becomes a sensual massage, compassion sliding into passion. Both domestic and exotic, funny and exciting, the peppermint foot lotion brings the comforts of home *and* transports the boys to a world of romantic fantasy. Strong but sweet, crude but also delicate ('I'm gonna stink of mint,' Ste says), the peppermint lotion stimulates the olfactory and the tactile senses, bringing Jamie and Ste together through touch and smell.

Jamie wants to extend these to sight, but when he asks Ste to turn over so that he can rub his front, Ste wants the lights turned off so that Jamie will not see his erection – and so that Ste himself will not have to recognise his own homosexual response. 'Do you think I'm queer?' Ste asks, clearly scared of being stigmatised by society, and, when Jamie wants to touch him, Ste replies with

'I'm a bit sore.' But this fearful refusal is also a plea for love, a call for Jamie to tend to Ste's heart and the rest of his body in the way that he has tended to his wounds, as Jamie realises when he goes on to touch Ste's face, to stroke his chest and then to move on down below. Although the actual event is elided – to keep the scene 'romantic'? to preserve the boys' 'innocence'? – it is clearly implied that 'Jamie and Ste have sex for the first time after the massage scene'.[69]

Brokeback Mountain (2005)

Director: Ang Lee
Cast: Jake Gyllenhaal (Jack), Heath Ledger (Ennis), Michelle Williams (Ennis's wife), Randy Quaid (the boss)

Wyoming 1963. Jack and Ennis are two cowboys who fall in love. It's tempting to think that, if Ennis had had the courage to declare his feelings for Jack and be seen as gay, the two men would have had the chance of a life together rather than trying to pass as straight and seeing each other only occasionally when they could leave their wives behind in town and reunite on Brokeback Mountain, where they first made love. While there is some truth to this view, it's important to recognise how extremely difficult it is for Ennis to speak up and come out as gay. As a boy, he was traumatised by seeing the bloody body of a gay cowboy who had been castrated in a homophobic lynching and left as a warning. He tells Jack that if the two of them are seen together 'in the wrong place in the wrong time', then 'we're dead'. Ennis fears that people are looking at him as if 'they all know', and, indeed, there seems to be no place or time where the men are free from judgemental eyes. Not only are they seen kissing in town by Ennis's wife, but even on Brokeback Mountain – a seemingly utopian setting for the natural expression of their love – the men are spotted in erotic horseplay by their boss through binoculars.

Because he sees himself through other people's eyes, Ennis cannot bear to recognise his own homosexuality, for, in society's view, to be gay is to be passive, effeminate, emasculated and victimised. This is one reason why, when Jack first makes sexual advances towards him, Ennis quickly takes charge and becomes the dominant one, bending Jack over and taking *him* anally. Even in the privacy of a mountain tent at night, Ennis must 'act the man' and not be 'feminised', for he has internalised society's negative view of gays. Jack recalls that, even in their non-sexual moments of hugging, Ennis 'would not then embrace him face to face because he did not want to see nor feel that it was Jack he held'.[70] To recognise that he is with a man would be for Ennis to acknowledge his own homosexuality and to view himself through society's eyes as contemptible.

Fear keeps Ennis closeted and *silenced*. At risk of condemnation and death, homosexuality is literally 'the love that dare not speak its name'. How can Ennis proclaim what he is when the only words for it are stigmatising and emasculating? 'Jack Twist?' Ennis's wife says with disgust, more like 'Jack *Nasty*' — for, in her view, the fact that Jack is male gives their love a 'nasty twist', making it a perversion. 'Twist,' their boss says to Jack, 'you guys wasn't gettin' paid to... stem the rose,' using an expression that mocks gay sex as effeminate (only ladies love flowers) and unspeakable except via euphemism (for anal penetration). Because homophobic paranoia is so pervasive, gay sex sometimes seems to be at once everywhere and nowhere, always heard (pejoratively) between the lines, though never actually (positively) spoken. Even Jack and Ennis's beloved 'Brokeback Mountain' can be heard as negative in linking homosexuality ('bareback mounting') to violence (a 'broken back') — heard by those who think that gay sex *is* violence (what 'real man' would want to be penetrated?) or that it will lead to violence (gay bashing and death). But it is equally possible, if one were so inclined, to hear homosexuality as resonating positively throughout the film, even in the very names of Jack and Ennis – Jack who moves Ennis's hand to his cock so his lover will 'jack' him off, and Ennis who enjoys penetrating Jack's 'anus'. Every time they speak their names, Jack and Ennis declare their desire – for those open to hearing it.

INCEST

Angels and Insects (1995)

Director: Philip Haas
Cast: Mark Rylance (William), Patsy Kensit (Eugenia), Douglas Henshall (Edgar)

1860s' England. Impoverished William is attracted to the aristocratic Eugenia Alabaster. They marry but, in the years that follow, he is only admitted to her room for sex during the times when she can conceive children, of which she proceeds to have many. One day, though, William returns unexpectedly to the country house and discovers Eugenia in bed with her brother Edgar. It turns out that the two of them have had a long-standing sexual liaison and that it is Edgar who sired all the children, in-breeding in order to keep the aristocratic family line 'pure'. William is understandably shocked and deeply injured by this revelation. The sight of Edgar's erect cock as he pulls away from Eugenia is ocular proof that William has been cuckolded, displaced as a husband and father by the 'bigger man'. William has also had impressed upon him his class inferiority, for he has been used as a mere pawn: his marriage to the 'queen' was a false front allowing Eugenia and her brother to carry on with their aristocratic affair. William had thought of the high-born Eugenia as a heavenly angel or a beautiful butterfly, but now he sees her colourful dresses, to which he was attracted, as a lure to draw him into her honey-trap, the sham of a marriage. Eugenia herself now seems more like a lowly insect, the incest she commits being a matter of base instinct and blind lust rather than the higher, human faculty of love.

But how humane is William when he roundly condemns ('You are disgusting'), repels ('I shan't touch you'), shames ('Why don't you just cover yourself?') and then abandons her? Eugenia tries to explain that the incest began when she was 'very little' and that, even later, when she tried to stop, her brother Edgar was 'strong!' Earlier, William had seen Edgar practically raping a housemaid, and yet William fails to recognise the extent to which Eugenia may have been psychologically and physically overpowered by her brutish brother from an early age. If only Eugenia could have spoken to someone about it, she might have been able to overcome the incest. But she was enjoined to silence on the subject from the very beginning, and when a former suitor found out about her secret, the fact that 'he could not speak it out loud' only reinforced her sense that it was too terrible to utter. Nevertheless, her body communicates her true feelings in its own way. When Eugenia is repulsed by a male moth that threatens to crawl under her dress, her fear of this invading insect conveys her loathing of incest.

And yet, 'taught' by her brother to be compliant and not really understanding what incest is or why it is wrong (since it is never spoken about), Eugenia continues to take Edgar into her bed. Since it started so early, incest was akin to masturbation – 'like touching yourself in the dark' – in the formation of her sexual identity, and, physiologically, she sometimes got pleasure from it: 'I know it was bad, but you must understand: it didn't *feel* bad.' One might wonder if it is Eugenia's ability to take pleasure in sex – something he does not expect from his Victorian 'angel' – that William finds disturbing, not just the incest. On their wedding night, he seems rather taken aback by her sexual knowledge – her ready participation in the act, her biting his shoulder at orgasm and her reaching for his cock the next morning. What William is unable to see is that Eugenia is neither a virginal angel nor an incestuous insect: she is a woman.

Pola X (1999)

Director: Leos Carax
Cast: Catherine Deneuve (Marie), Guillaume Depardieu (Pierre), Delphine Chuillot (Lucie), Yekaterina Golubeva (Isabelle)

With their matching *E* names, blond hair and red riding coats, Edgar and Eugenia – the aristocratic Alabasters in *Angels and Insects* – interbred incestuously to reinforce the family lineage against outsiders. Similarly, in *Pola X*, Marie wants her son Pierre to marry Lucie, whose inherited wealth and beauty make her the mother's younger double. In fact, Marie and Lucie are often seen from behind, with their blonde hair making them almost interchangeable. In the film's first scene, a naked Pierre slips into a bed where a blonde woman is lying face-down and takes her from behind. The woman is Lucie, but we don't know this yet and, even when we do find out, the sense remains that it might be someone else, someone equally 'golden' – rich and blonde – like Marie. Later, as Lucie is in the middle of pulling a shirt off over her head, Pierre stops her and kisses her face through the shirt. As before with the sex from behind, the interaction is anonymous and hardly qualifies as true contact, for it is neither directly physical nor really personal. It is more the *idea* of 'the family, the couple, the power of love' than its *actuality*, for it could be any woman that Pierre is almost kissing here. And, as Lucie tilts her shirt-bound arms and head back in exaggerated enjoyment, it is more the *idea* of a handsome, moneyed man that excites her than any *reality* of his touch. The fact that the shirt-bound Lucie looks like the writhing victim in a sado-masochistic scenario is a comment on the perversity of her and Pierre's 'love', which is narcissistically enraptured with wealth and power.

If Pierre's sex with Lucie involves a kind of aristocratic in-breeding, then his lovemaking with his half-sister Isabelle is also incestuous, but in a very different way. The offspring of an affair that Pierre's father once had, Isabelle was repudiated by Marie as illegitimate and exiled from the ancestral home, but now Isabelle has returned from war-torn Bosnia to seek the help of her only living blood relation, Pierre. The black sheep of the family, Isabelle has dark tangled hair unlike the golden locks of Marie and Lucie. Isabelle's hair often obscures her face and, rejected by family and society, she has been forced into homeless vagrancy, sometimes squatting in dark and abandoned buildings. Pierre's sex with Isabelle is a reconnection with the half-sister he barely knew when they were young before she was forcibly separated from him and her home. Pierre fleshes out the idea of a loving couple through passionate coupling with Isabelle. The two of them lock lips in a face-to-face kiss, and their physical contact is graphically depicted by shots of his hand between her legs, her mouth taking him in and his cock penetrating her cunt as she rides him to a mutual orgasm. Intertwined in the darkness, brother and half-sister become almost indistinguishable, blood relations reunited as if they were one body. Afterwards, they sleep facing each other like mirror images folding inward. In another shot of them asleep, we see her vagina in the foreground as, turned on her stomach, she rests her head and dark hair on his crotch while he lies in the background, his head out of frame. Incest has brought them together, but it has also reduced them to mere bodies conjoined in lust outside of the conjugal rite of marriage. Disowned and shoved into obscurity, Isabelle and Pierre have no family name or social standing and thus no stable sense of self which would be needed to form a lasting relationship. All they have is their intimate physical connection, like the bond between twin siblings in the womb, and this is not enough for them to live in the larger world – as evidenced by Pierre's prophetic dream of clinging to Isabelle while the two of them drown in a river of blood.

Savage Grace (2007)

Director: Tom Kalin
Cast: Julianne Moore (Barbara), Eddie Redmayne (Tony), Stephen Dillane (Brooks)

Near the end of *Savage Grace*, a mother named Barbara sits down next to her son Tony on the sofa. She tells him that he shouldn't be seeing a lot of one of his gay friends 'if what you want to learn is how to be a man'. The sex that Barbara is about to have with Tony is thus partly a maternal attempt to instruct her son in how to be a heterosexual man. It's worth pointing out that, in this, Barbara is taking on a role which she feels has been vacated by the boy's father: not only has Brooks left Tony and her, but she fears that Brooks, too, may be a homosexual and thus not a 'proper' role model for Tony, so she must take on that part. Barbara puts her hand on Tony's leg, saying that she very much likes the fabric. In complimenting his taste in clothes – a taste that she had a hand in forming, Barbara is approving the kind of man that Tony is growing up to be, a man who wears his wealth well ('clothes make the man'). Barbara's immigrant mother had taught her to 'find the mon', by which she meant a man with money, and Barbara tried to follow this advice by marrying Brooks, but he left her and so now the 'mon' she has is Tony.

When she moves her hand up his thigh, asking what his pants fabric is called, he says 'It's a worsted, I should think,' closing his legs a bit and turning his head briefly away from her. In these ways, Tony tries to keep his head ('I should think') and to tell his mother that what she's doing is wrong (it is the 'worst' sort of behaviour). However, when Barbara proceeds to stroke his crotch, noting that 'part of you doesn't seem to mind it', he lets his physiological response overrule his moral qualms, opening his legs to her and saying, 'I suppose I don't – mind.' Barbara straddles him on the sofa and puts him inside her, asking 'How does that feel?' Tony's reply – 'I think you know' – is ambiguous and ambivalent. She knows it feels good to him because it feels good to her: each of them gets sexual pleasure, along with enjoyment in seeing that the other does, too. But Tony's words are also an implied accusation: it is precisely because they know each other so well, because they are members of the same family, that he should not be inside her. From her pregnancy, she already knows what it feels like to have him in her womb, which is the only right way for a mother to be with her child. What Barbara should be feeling now, as she has sex with her son, is the same shame that Tony is feeling, and his words are an attempt to tell her so.

Yet Barbara rides Tony up and down on the sofa, panting with her eyes closed and his face obscured by her shoulder in one shot. Intent on her own pleasure, she doesn't even see him. She lets her own sexual desires blind her to the shame her son is feeling. She lets her own needs overshadow his, which are for maternal care, not sensual satisfaction. Ironically, after her orgasm, Barbara is concerned that Tony hasn't come, so she masturbates him to ejaculation. Afterwards, Tony sits with his thumb in his mouth, curled up in a near-foetal position on the kitchen floor. Rather than making him into a man, the sex his mother had with him has caused him to regress to an infantile state, seeking the nourishment – the care and affection – he was unable to get from her.

Beautiful Kate (2009)

Director: Rachel Ward
Cast: Scott O'Donnell (Ned), Sophie Lowe (Kate)

With their mother deceased and their father emotionally distant, Ned and Kate are twins 'going through puberty in isolation' on their family farm in the remote Australian outback.[71] One day, Ned walks half-naked into the bathroom and, standing in his bulging white briefs behind Kate, sees her putting vapour rub on her bare breasts. She shouts angrily for him to get out. Later, she enters his bedroom covered in a white towel and shares her fears of growing old, saying that she liked things better when the two of them were young. She asks him to tickle her (the way they used to do as kids) and he lies in bed behind her, walking his fingers over her back in their old game of jungle explorer. When he wonders if the vapour rub was for a cold, she replies that she just likes the smell of it because it reminds her of their mother. Kate cries and Ned embraces her from behind, rubbing her arm to comfort her. However, he then grips her arm, groaning, and she reaches behind and sits up, staring at the semen in her hand and realising that he has inadvertently ejaculated, about which he feels mortified. This scene shows Kate on a backwards trajectory, wanting to 'recover the lost intimacies of [their] childhood together', to return to a time when she and her brother were 'twined... as in [their] mother's womb'.[72] For her, the vapour rub and Ned's rubbing are primarily asexual forms of contact associated with sibling closeness and maternal care. But for Ned, who is on a forwards trajectory of sexual exploration, the naked contact with his sister's developing body elicits an erotic response over and against his countervailing wish to be a brother (or a mother) to her.

In a later scene, after agreeing to 'just pretend it never happened', Ned and Kate play happily together in the yard, where he stands holding a water hose at crotch-level and sprays her with it while she is lying on her back. Halfway between childish pleasure and adult desire, this scene seems poised between innocence and incest, and it is not clear how either he or she experiences it. Is it the pure opposite of that earlier ejaculation, or is it a disguised version of the same?

Still feeling guilty about the earlier incident, Ned gets drunk and jumps into the family dam, or pond. Despite his protest, Kate strips naked and jumps in as well, exclaiming that 'It's my dam, too!' Sharing her fear that her lack of interest in other boys means that she is not 'normal', Kate tells Ned that his desire for her makes her feel better and less like a 'freak'. She brings his hands to her breasts, saying 'You can touch them, Neddy. It'll be our secret.' She kisses him, and the two of them make out passionately in the water, followed by intercourse to mutual orgasm on the banks of the dam. Afterwards, he is again guilt-stricken and remorseful, but she is quite happy, singing a childish song as she washes herself in the pond. For Kate, incest is both a regression to the past and an attempt at future growth. By entwining with Ned in the 'dam' (which is also a word for 'mother'), she rejoins him in the womb. However, Ned could also be a transitional figure for her on the way to other boys. If she can desire him in the way that he does her, maybe that mutual desire is possible with others, too. Incest may ironically be Kate's attempt to emerge from the womb/dam and climb its banks, to give birth to herself as a mature woman. Rather than making her a 'freak', incest seems to be the means by which Kate hopes to become 'normal'.

INFIDELITY

Last Tango in Paris (1972)

Director: Bernardo Bertolucci
Cast: Maria Schneider (Jeanne), Jean-Pierre Léaud (Tom), Marlon Brando (Paul)

Jeanne is engaged to Tom, so why is she unfaithful to him, repeatedly running off to have sex with Paul? Tom is an idealistic filmmaker who insists that Jeanne act the role of his romantic counterpart in the true-life 'love story' he is shooting about them. However, the fact that every 'kiss' and 'caress' is for 'cinema' suggests that it is all for show, a social act without individual validity. When Jeanne makes the personal decision to change her hair, Tom is disturbed by the lack of continuity, implying that he expects her to stay the same, to fit her rehearsed role as his wife and not to improvise. Being fitted for the wedding, Jeanne comments obliquely on its social constraint ('It's the dress that makes the bride'), while noting that theirs is to be an 'advertising marriage' where she has to be 'smiling' like the woman 'in the posters'.

Her time with Paul is different, as shown in the scene where she slowly lifts her white wedding dress to reveal her naked black pubic bush underneath. With Paul, she can display her personal desires and satisfy some of the basic urges that she is otherwise expected to repress as a virginal bride and a 'good little wife', who has sex only for procreation. In their very first erotic encounter, Paul throws her fancy hat away, rips off her underwear and screws her standing up with her back against a window, acting in lustful defiance of social convention. Paul doesn't give a damn about the outside world – he doesn't want to know anything about her, not even her name. This frees her to be herself, to return to a time of childhood sexual discovery before shame or inhibition, as when the two of them sit naked together and she comments, 'It's beautiful without knowing anything. Maybe we can come without touching.' Here Jeanne recreates the idyllic past when she and her cousin (also named Paul), both in their early teens, sat under separate trees in an Edenic garden and masturbated in front of each other, playing a game in which the first to come won. If only sex could always be like this, playful yet meaningful, innocent yet passionate, preserving individuality while allowing for togetherness.

But sex with Paul also unearths memories of more disturbing aspects of Jeanne's past. When he asks her if he can open the 'hiding place' between her legs, she demurs, indicating that 'maybe there's some family secrets inside'. One such secret is that Jeanne's father, a colonel in the French army, had adulterous relations with a young native woman while he was stationed in Algeria. The father she idolised ('I loved him like a god – he was so handsome in his uniform') is thus revealed to have had a false front ('All uniforms are bullshit,' says Paul): behind the respectable bourgeois, there was a lustful savage. Paul, who is old enough to be Jeanne's father, sometimes behaves like a brute, as when he forcibly sodomises her while making her mock 'the family' as 'a holy institution meant to breed virtue in savages'. And yet Jeanne keeps coming back to him ('I wanted to leave you and I couldn't – I can't!'), with part of her even seeming to enjoy being mistreated. Could she be drawn to Paul because his passionate abuse reminds her of what her father did to her as a child, a terrible 'love' that she both fears and craves? Could that be the other 'family secret' buried in her? 'I'm Little Red Riding Hood and you're the wolf,' says Jeanne as she lifts the bedsheets to uncover the various parts of Paul's body, including his furry chest and his penis, the way she might have done with her father. But when she tries to idealise her childhood as 'the most beautiful thing', Paul becomes ferocious, causing her to realise how her father used her admiration for him and her innocence to abuse her: 'Is it beautiful... to be forced to admire authority or sell yourself for a piece of candy?' In another scene, Jeanne holds her father's military pistol, saying that 'It used to seem so heavy when I was little, and Papa was teaching me to shoot it' – a statement that hints at childhood sexual abuse. At the end of the film, Jeanne uses this same pistol to shoot Paul, who has donned her father's military cap and is trying to press himself upon her. In this way, she protects herself against an abusive man – the way her father should have done.

Breaking the Waves (1996)

Director: Lars von Trier
Cast: Emily Watson (Bess), Stellan Skarsgård (Jan)

Pious, virginal Bess finds pleasure in the flesh for the first time with her husband Jan. Right after they are married by the church, Bess has him meet her in the bathroom at the reception where she lifts up her wedding dress, slips off her underwear and has Jan take her up against a wall. Later, as he's lying naked in bed, she touches his body in wonder and collapses in joyous laughter when she reaches his cock. Then, as he is thrusting on top of her, she smiles and looks heavenward, giving thanks to God, which she also does in church: 'I thank you for the greatest gift of all, the gift of love. I thank you for Jan.' When the two are separated because Jan must work on an oil rig out in the ocean, they stay in touch via phone sex, a kind of ethereal connection that is also still very physical as Bess tells him, 'I'm touching your arms and your chest and your tummy and your prick. You're so huge!'

But then Jan has an accident on the rig and is paralysed from the neck down, rendering him impotent. Believing that his young wife will wither without physical love, Jan bids her to have sex with other men and to come tell him about it as a way to keep him alive. This she does, reporting back to him about one of her encounters that 'I go to the back of the bus and you are there, and you're so huge that you're almost bursting out of your pants, and I undo your fly and I touch you, I'm touching your prick.' It is possible that Bess's 'stories about being in love' could have succeeded, as the phone sex did before, at maintaining their marital connection. Jan could have *taken pleasure* in hearing them, in having his ears and heart and soul respond like sex organs, in having his manhood reaffirmed and his wife's continuing love for him confirmed by proxy. For her part, Bess might have been able to *enjoy* sex with other men, to believe that feeling physical pleasure with them is continuous with the joy she has found with her husband, a way of strengthening the holy bonds of matrimony. Instead, listening to Bess's stories provokes only pain in Jan, who feels sexually betrayed by his wife as well as impotent and inferior to these other men – even though he asked her to go with them! And Bess experiences her extramarital encounters as sordid and sinful, as when she keeps her eyes tightly closed while jerking off a man on the bus and then vomits in disgust, or when she submits to rough sex with a sailor who ends up using his knife on her body. The pious Bess feels that she must mortify her flesh in order to remain spiritually faithful to her husband.

In the end, Jan miraculously walks again and heavenly bells ring out in apparent approval of Bess's sacrifice. But must spiritual happiness be bought at the price of physical suffering? Why can't heavenly joy and sensual pleasure go together, as they seemed to when Jan and Bess first got married? 'We do not need bells in our church to worship God,' a minister tells Bess, and her reply is that 'I like church bells. Let's put them back again.' Indeed. Why is the thought of spiritual and sexual joy – of bells and balls – so profane and ridiculous? Why can't spirit be loved as embodied in flesh?

Little Children (2006)

Director: Todd Field
Cast: Kate Winslet (Sarah), Patrick Wilson (Brad)

Sarah is a stay-at-home mom tending to her daughter while her husband is away at his job, and Brad is a suburban 'househusband' raising his son while his wife works in the city. As they are watching their kids at a neighbourhood playground, Sarah impulsively kisses Brad to prove that she is not just another suburban mom. The sexual charge of their kiss comes in part from this defiance, from how shocked the other mothers are at this indiscretion. Sarah and Brad are behaving more like naughty children than like responsible adults. Then, at the public pool, Sarah uses her daughter's need for shade as a pretext to sit near Brad and his son, and the sun ('Hot enough for you?') becomes Sarah's excuse to have Brad rub suntan lotion on her back, while her daughter sings innocently, 'Who is knocking on the door?' Later, as their kids nap together in another room, Brad and Sarah get together in the basement where, after loading the tumble dryer with clothes like a good mother, she sits naked on a sink counter and opens her legs to him while he stands and thrusts into her. As Kate Winslet (who plays Sarah) has said, 'That precious core of her identity is lost somewhere within her' and 'she wants to uncover it';[73] 'Sarah really comes out of herself and changes as a result of being in that physical position where she's feeling something that she's never felt before.'[74] Adulterous passion with Brad allows Sarah access to her physical being, the sexual part so essential to her identity that it is her 'precious core'. The asexual role of caring mother, while vitally important to her as well, has covered up the other part, alienating her from her sensual self. It would seem that Sarah became filled with child before she ever had a chance to find sexual fulfilment. It is through this adulterous affair that she herself becomes a child again, 'feeling something that she's never felt before', discovering the physical pleasure that she missed when she became an adult too soon.

Brad, too, is rejuvenated by the affair. More than just an illicit thrill, sex with Sarah makes him feel like a virile youth and no longer emasculated by his working wife who 'wears the pants in the family'. Sarah admires his hard body and desires his cock, always reaching for it to go another round and making him feel everlastingly potent. But the sex brings with it an emotional intimacy that is just as important. Brad's mother died when he was only a boy and now his wife seems to lavish all her attention on their son. With Sarah, Brad can *be* the child who gets his mother all to himself, who finally gets the mothering he missed when he lost his own. In one lovemaking sequence, after vigorously fucking her up against a wall, Brad slips Sarah's bra strap off her shoulders and moves his mouth to her breast. (The novel has him ask, 'Mind if I suck your breast?')[75] Brad can be both virile and vulnerable with her, for she is a lover and a mother to him, in a sense birthing him into manhood. When he is nervous about failing at football (a game he hasn't played in years), Sarah tells him he'll be great, and after Brad scores the winning touchdown, he scores with her, too, making out with her on the football field:

'For the first time in my life, I feel like anything is possible, like I can do anything.'

And yet, according to the film's ending, Brad and Sarah must renounce their relationship for the sake of their families. The two must stop parenting each other as children and be parents to their own. It would seem that it's too late for Sarah to be a lover *and* a mother, too late for Brad to be a father *and* a lover. However, if the love the two briefly found together can be nurtured in their own children, it may not be too late for *them*.

The Night Buffalo (El búfalo de la noche) (2007)

Director: Jorge Hernández Aldana
Cast: Gabriel González (Gregorio), Liz Gallardo (Tania), Diego Luna (Manuel)

Gregorio is in and out of a mental hospital for schizophrenia while, behind his back, his girlfriend Tania and his best friend Manuel are sleeping with each other. Gregorio commits suicide with a gunshot to the head. Before this, he had bloodily amputated two toes in an effort to get rid of the earwigs he felt were eating him up inside. So close to him, Manuel and Tania were like parts of Gregorio's own body which he had to 'cut off' because his suspicion of their affair was destroying him. After the suicide, Manuel receives a box of mementos left for him by Gregorio, out of which comes an earwig that crawls on Manuel. Manuel had convinced Tania that they weren't really betraying Gregorio because he was insane, but as the two embrace and she professes to love Manuel, he can't help but whisper in her ear: 'More than Gregorio?' If Tania can cheat on Gregorio with Manuel, then couldn't she betray Manuel, too? The 'earwig' of doubt has passed from Gregorio to Manuel and Tania, for their infidelity to him has led them to suspect that they could be similarly unfaithful to each other. Tania remembers a terrified Gregorio pushing her away from him in bed, saying 'Don't touch me! ...The earwigs are eating me up! ...You could catch them!' Now she, too, is devoured by doubt, as Manuel's suspicions of her fill her with jealousy about who *he* might be sleeping with. And, indeed, as the two grow more and more estranged, Manuel does have sex with other women, all of whom look like Tania, much as she slept with Manuel who looks very much like Gregorio. The film jumps back and forth between past and present, and the lovemaking scenes are shot with an emphasis on body parts and with the characters' faces turned away or obscured by hair or shadow, so it is often hard to tell who is in bed with whom: Gregorio with Tania, Manuel with Tania, Manuel with a Tania lookalike, Tania with some other man? As Manuel thinks about Tania in the novel, 'I was suddenly overcome by the anxiety of not knowing who she really was or where she was going.'[76]

After Manuel and Tania first made love, she tore out a patch of the blood-spotted bed-sheet to prove that she had given her virginity to him, asking him to 'never forget' that he's the one she loves. But is blood proof enough? Manuel and Gregorio had gotten matching buffalo tattoos on their arms, using the same needle to prove that they would be 'blood brothers'. But Gregorio was betrayed by Manuel, as Manuel could be by Tania. Was Manuel already sleeping with her before he and Gregorio became blood brothers? Had Tania already given her virginity and her true love to Gregorio before sleeping with Manuel? For Manuel, the betrayer betrayed, doubt is *always already inside him*, like a part of his own body that he thought he could love and trust, but which has turned against him and must be amputated because it is destroying him. Looking into a mirror, Manuel takes a knife to the tattoo in a bloody attempt to cut it out of his arm. But his conscience will not let him deny his blood bond with the friend he effectively killed with his betrayal – Gregorio who, with his matching buffalo tattoo, in effect stares back at Manuel from the mirror, mocking Manuel's efforts to cut him out of his life.

The buffalo that Gregorio used to feel breathing on him while he slept was his terrifying intuition of his best friend's betrayal. Now, because of his infidelity, Manuel will remain forever suspicious of others *and himself*. As Gregorio told him, 'Now the night buffalo will dream about you.'

Incendiary (2008)

Director: Sharon Maguire
Cast: Michelle Williams (Young Mother), Ewan McGregor (Jasper)

Our main character – a young woman whose name we never learn – has no identity beyond that of wife and mother. Although she dearly loves her two 'chaps', her husband is physically and emotionally distant, his life consumed by work, and she is almost too close to her four-year-old son, her life absorbed into his. One day, when her husband and son are away at a football match, she goes back to her apartment with a neighbour, Jasper, who listens – and makes love – to her. Their sexual moves are counterpointed by the plays of the football game as these are announced on the TV in the living room where the two are going at it on the sofa. After the longing looks and the flirtatious talk ('We've been looking forward to this game for a long time, but now the talking is over and the action begins'), he and she engage in a variety of positions which culminate with him on top, moving inside her ('Another promising-looking attack and that's a superb ball in'). During this scene, the young woman is able to imagine having it all: she can achieve her own fulfilment while her husband and son enjoy one of the supreme pleasures in their life, the football match. For once, their enjoyment does not come at the cost of hers; instead, she can imagine their cheering her on as if they approved her having a life for herself and not just one lived for them: '[one player's] shot went in sweet and low and so did Jasper... the crowd went wild. ...I knew my husband and my boy were singing their hearts out there on the East Stand. They would of been feeling great. I was feeling great too. ...Jasper was moving quicker inside me it was obvious Arsenal were going to score again I was going to explode.'[77]

However, at the moment that she 'explodes' in orgasm, a bomb goes off at the football stadium, killing hundreds including her husband and her son. The dream of total fulfilment has become a nightmare in which her taking some female pleasure for herself ends up killing her family. Her husband was actually a policeman who worked in bomb disposal, and she had spent many days in terrible worry that he would not come home. Now she herself seems to have brought about the very thing she most feared, her infidelity having 'triggered' his death. In the days before the explosion, she had looked out her window and across the street to see Jasper enter his house with another woman, whose carefree single life of sexual freedom she had envied. Now, in 'trying on' that life through her brief affair with Jasper, in imagining herself free for a moment of amorous dalliance and not tied to her husband or son, she seems to have *wiped them out*, vaporising them as if they had never existed. Blaming herself for their deaths, she won't let Jasper touch her, not even to comfort her. 'I'm not a good or decent person,' she says, believing that 'I have murdered love'. She prays for death to take her, too – both as punishment for her 'incendiary' desires and in desperate hope of being with her family again.

But then the young woman discovers a reason to live when she finds herself pregnant with a son, who was probably conceived on that day with Jasper. Some viewers may see this as a sign that she will once more be living *for someone else* and not for herself: has her son been 'returned' to her on condition that she never again seek to satisfy her own desires? However, since the boy is a product of her attempt at sexual fulfilment, perhaps he is a sign of a better future – one where being a loving wife and mother is not incompatible with a passion of her own.

Chloe (2009)

Director: Atom Egoyan
Cast: Julianne Moore (Catherine), Liam Neeson (David), Amanda Seyfried (Chloe)

Catherine suspects her husband David is cheating, so she hires a prostitute, Chloe, to tempt him and find out. As Chloe reports back details of her increasingly intimate encounters with David, Catherine keeps wanting her to take it further, ostensibly to see how far David will go and to rediscover what he likes in a woman, since he no longer seems attracted to her. Jealousy appears to excite Catherine as she listens to the accounts of what Chloe and David do together, but it becomes less and less certain *whom* Catherine is *jealous of* and whether she wants their 'affair' to continue because it brings her closer to David or *to Chloe*. While remembering what Chloe said about going down on David, Catherine brings the shower head down her body until the spray is turned on her sex, and her hand trembles in ecstasy as she heard that David's did. In another scene, Chloe puts lotion on Catherine's hands – Catherine who 'loved [David's] hands. They used to grab me everywhere.' Then, in a hotel room where Chloe says David made love to her, Catherine uses her hands to open Chloe's blouse and bare her breasts, asking, 'How does he touch you?' As writer Erin Cressida Wilson says, Catherine 'needs to feel desire and she wants, she's becoming her husband and feeling what her husband feels and coming into her own as a woman, through Chloe'.[78] In the hotel bed together, when Chloe kisses Catherine's breasts and works a hand between her legs, bringing her to orgasm, is it the thought of being with her husband – or of being her husband with Chloe, of *being with Chloe* – that excites Catherine? When it's discovered that Chloe has never actually been with David, that she has merely been making up stories about the two of them, Catherine is revealed as the one who had the true erotic encounter with Chloe. Catherine is 'the only one cheating, and she's the only one hiring hookers'.[79]

After their lovemaking in the hotel bed, Catherine withdraws from Chloe, claiming that theirs was a financial transaction and that whatever Catherine felt was for her husband. Chloe perseveres – 'I don't want this to be over, and I don't think that you want it to be, either. ...I touched you' – and, when rejected, acts like a jilted lover and threatens Catherine's family and her life. After Catherine pushes her away in self-defence, Chloe falls to her death. The film ends with a scene where Catherine and David exchange meaningful glances, their marriage restored, and we see that Catherine has her hair pinned up, held together by a hair clasp which Chloe had given her as a token of their love. Catherine's sexual energy is now bound to her husband, held within the marital bond, but it was Chloe who freed her desire, who exceeded the terms of *their* contract and deeply 'touched' Catherine. As happy as Catherine may be in her lawful marriage to David, a melancholy part of her must mourn the loss of Chloe and their 'illicit' love. Catherine may also miss those times of being with David through Chloe, of being like David with Chloe – those times of desire unbound.

Mirch (2010)

Director: Vinay Shukla
Cast: Rajpal Yadav (Kashi), Raima Sen (Maya), Arunoday Singh (Madho)

Mirch, which its director has described as 'India's first film in the erotic genre',[80] presents four stories and a frame tale connected by the common theme of adultery. The first story, which will be our focus here, is set in ancient India and based on a folktale from the *Panchatantra* about a carpenter (Kashi) who suspects his wife (Maya) of infidelity. However, unlike the source text, which bluntly condemns its female character from the start ('His wife was a whore, and reputed to be such'),[81] the film strongly suggests that whatever faults the wife has can be traced back to her husband. Though she prepares delicious dishes for him every day (as seen in a sultry shot of moisture beading Maya's neck while she kneads dough), Kashi suspects that some of these meals must be for other men whom she 'serves' behind his back while he is out working. It is Kashi's own sense of inferiority that leads him to doubt that she could ever lavish such loving attention solely on him. Similarly, because he feels unworthy of it, his wife's very desire for him becomes in Kashi's mind the proof that she must yearn for another. Thus, when she sings – 'What is this fever that burns me? Oh, my lover, you slake this fire' – and runs her fingers seductively over the bare soles of his feet, he moves them away, denying her the love she craves because he fears she is singing of someone else. The insecure Kashi lets his fears be fed by gossip concerning Maya's 'affairs' – rumours spread by Kashi's co-worker Madho who wants to have an affair with her and so may hope they come true. 'Suspicion bites me like a venomous snake,' thinks Kashi, who succumbs to belief in the worst of society's stereotypes about women: 'Maya is illusion and so deceitful by nature.'

Resolving to test his wife, Kashi lies to her about a faraway job, causing her pain over their 'need' to part, then doubles back and hides under the bed, waiting for her to receive her lover there. Kashi thus combines the sins of dishonesty, desertion and stealth. Sure enough – and not surprisingly after all he has done to make it a self-fulfilling prophecy, Maya does take a lover: Madho, who lies on top of the bed under which Kashi is hiding, which emphasises the fact that Madho is Kashi's double and replacement, the lover she took *because* her husband had withdrawn from her. Whereas Kashi had pulled his away, Madho runs his bare foot up Maya's body. Kashi's response is to hold a knife up, all his sexual energy turned to jealous rage. Maya then tells an elaborate lie that uses Kashi's negative stereotyping of her to her own advantage. According to a prophecy, she says, Kashi is soon to die, but if Maya can find a lover who will take her husband's place in bed with her, death may pass to the other man, and Kashi may be saved. In this way, Maya takes her husband's fears concerning her – that she is a faithless whore and that a man 'may die after sexual union with' her – and uses them to get what she wants. Maya and her lover proceed to have sex on the bed right above Kashi, who is so egotistically glad to be 'saved from death' that he rejoices in his own cuckolding!

INTERRACIAL

The Lover (L'amant) (1992)

Director: Jean-Jacques Annaud
Cast: Jane March (The Girl), Tony Leung (The Man)

1929 French Indochina. A girl who is 15½, poor and French has a forbidden love affair with a man who is 32, rich and Chinese. (The two characters are unnamed, but we will call them the Girl and the Man.) The Man comments approvingly on a man's fedora hat that the Girl always wears. Her relationship with this older Man is perhaps related to the hat in being a way for her to recapture a closeness to her father, who has died. It is a way for her to imagine being 'fathered' into maturity, being safely and lovingly brought from girlhood into womanhood. The racial gap between them adds to the age difference in making him seem more 'other' to her, more like a father than the kind of boy she would be expected to date. At the same time, the man's hat she wears suggests a certain 'masculinity' in the Girl, who ultimately takes the initiative in having sex with the Man. While he begins in conventionally aggressive fashion by tearing her dress and underpants off and carrying her to bed, fear overcomes him and so she is the one who undresses and makes love to him. As she runs her hand down his body, she feels that his 'skin is of a sumptuous softness' and that his 'body is hairless, without any virility at all other than that of the sex'. As she takes his penis in hand, she 'caresses the golden hue, the unknown novelty'. Part of what the Girl desires in this Man is a 'feminine' absence of hardness and hairiness – a soft and yellow skin, a languorous yielding to *her* advances, which she associates with his being Chinese. Unlike the macho thrusting of some hirsute Frenchman (such as the Girl's rapacious brother who seems a constant threat to her), the Chinese Man's lovemaking is gentle and tender, even when she allows him to take her virginity.

For her, sex with him is a synaesthetic experience of lying with her body open to the world, of loving the unknown sounds and smells of the Chinese district just outside the room where they make love: 'the smell of soup, roast meat, jasmine, dust, charcoal fire' – 'the smell of the Chinese town'. The Girl tastes him as they tongue-kiss. (Earlier, when offended by him at a restaurant, she had claimed that 'I don't like Chinese very much' – even as she was ravenously eating Chinese food!) She reaches her hand down to feel what is between his legs, unafraid to touch the unknown, thinking of 'the pleasure' she has found in 'this dark man from China'. Then she stretches her naked body out on top of his, making ecstatic contact with his 'otherness' at every point, rather than just being 'topped' by a man from her own culture, someone who she knows all too well would take his own pleasure and go.

Storytelling (2001)

Director: Todd Solondz
Cast: Selma Blair (Vi), Robert Wisdom (Mr Scott)

Vi, a student at a white liberal arts college, goes with her black creative writing teacher back to his apartment, where he has rough anal sex with her. She then writes a story about the incident, which is interpreted in different ways by other students in the writing workshop. According to director Todd Solondz, 'It's sort of a *Rashomon* thing,' but he then hastens to add: 'It is not a rape. It could never be construed as a rape.'[82] The female character's claim in *Rashomon* is that she was raped, so if Solondz disallows this possible reading of *Storytelling*, it is hard to see his film as being that much like *Rashomon*. Actress Selma Blair, who plays Vi, appears at first to have thought that 'rape' might be the correct word for what happens to her character, but then Blair seems to have moved towards a different interpretation: 'I viewed the scene as a little more of a rape than it seems now. But she's a consenting adult. ...She's a little girl who got in over her head.'[83] Is Vi a 'little girl' or a 'consenting adult'? If the scene now appears to be a little less of a rape, does that mean it's not rape? Blair still seems uncertain about how to define what happens to her character in the film.

In a bar before going to his apartment, Vi tells Mr Scott that 'I have so much respect for you.' She respects him as a professor, as an authority on black experience and as a Pulitzer Prize-winning writer. If her declaration of respect is also a pick-up line, it is no less genuine for that: she wants to be with the man she idolises. In the bathroom of his apartment, Vi finds nude photos of a white female classmate tied up in various positions. Rather than run screaming from the place, Vi tells herself, 'Don't be a racist.' This young student wants to do the right thing – elsewhere we see her wearing 'USA Africa' and 'Biko Lives' T-shirts – and she does not want to prejudicially condemn the actions of the man who wrote *A Sunday Lynching*, a man who may have his own reasons beyond her ken for tying up those white women. It's possible she thinks she can somehow make reparation as a loving sacrifice for the wrongs her race has done to his. In the bedroom where he is still clothed, he tells her to undress and she stands fully exposed to him, insecurely offering herself in the hope of his approval, much as she offered him her stories in the writing workshop. Lit

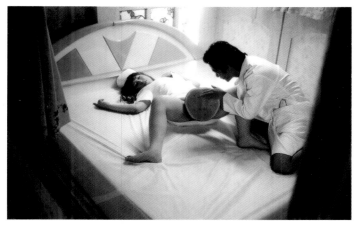

The Wayward Cloud (2005) directed by Ming-Liang Tsai. Wild Bunch.

Enter the Void (2009) directed by Gaspar Noé. Wild Bunch.

Shame (2011) directed by Steve McQueen. Fox Searchlight Pictures.

Cashback (2006) directed by Sean Ellis. Magnolia.

Little Children (2006) directed by Todd Field. New Line Cinema.

Shortbus (2006) directed by John Cameron Mitchell. TH!NKFilm.

Lie with Me (2005) directed by Clément Virgo. Conquering Lion.

9 Songs (2004) directed by Michael Winterbottom. Tartan.

Y Tu Mamá También (2001) directed by Alfonso Cuarón. Producciones Anhelo.

Clockwise from top left: *Splice* (2009) directed by Vincenzo Natali. Warner Bros. *The Brown Bunny* (2003) directed by Vincent Gallo. Vincent Gallo Productions. *Killing Me Softly* (2002) directed by Kaige Chen. Metro-Goldwyn-Mayer.

Chloe (2009) directed by Atom Egoyan. Sony.

Mirch (2010) directed by Vinay Shukla. Reliance Big.

The Notorious Bettie Page (2005) directed by Mary Harron. Picturehouse.

Clockwise from top left: *The Attendant* (1993) directed by Isaac Julien. British Film Institute. *Secretary* (2002) directed by Steven Shainberg. Slough Pond. *Forgetting Sarah Marshall* (2008) directed by Nicholas Stoller. Universal.

The Night Porter (1974) directed by Liliana Cavani. AVCO Embassy Pictures.

Lolita (1997) directed by Adrian Lyne. Pathé.

Ken Park (2002) directed by Larry Clark. Cinéa.

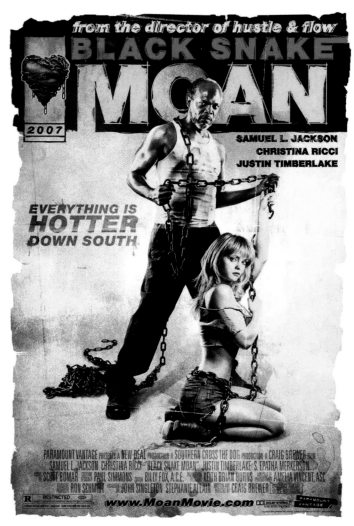

Black Snake Moan (2006) directed by Craig Brewer. Paramount.

by a lamp, her white skin and blonde hair contrast sharply with the dark silhouette he forms as he looms over her, yet she takes a step towards him, unafraid to bridge the racial gap.

However, instead of taking her into his arms for a kiss, Mr Scott has her turn around and bend over, where he proceeds to bugger her against the wall, ordering her to repeat the words 'Nigger, fuck me hard!' We cannot know how Vi feels about this act. She does not tell him 'no' or try to get him to stop. As she writes in her story later, she 'said what he asked her to say and did what he asked her to do'. It's possible that Vi is excited, along with Mr Scott, by this taboo-breaking fantasy of a black man having sex with a white woman, by the myth of black male potency and the forbidden thrill of succumbing to such an overpowering force. Or maybe she empathises with his pain and understands at some level that he is acting out his rage at racial injustice by using her. But there is also the possibility that she isn't excited and that she doesn't understand – that she is traumatised and betrayed by a man she opened herself up to and tried to connect with across the gender and racial divide. In her story, Vi writes about her sense of humiliation and degradation: 'She had entered college with hope, with dignity, but she would graduate as a whore.' In considering how she feels, we could take her at her word.

Black Snake Moan (2006)

Director: Craig Brewer
Cast: Samuel L Jackson (Lazarus), Christina Ricci (Rae)

Lazarus, a black Tennessee farmer, finds a young white woman, Rae, lying beaten and half-naked in the road outside his house. He carries her inside and, after finding out that she wants to run away and sleep with other men like the ones who left her for dead, he chains her to the radiator. This act is the basis for the film's notorious poster, which shows Rae, wearing nothing but a cropped top and a jeans skirt, wrapped in a big chain which is being held by Lazarus, who towers above her in his wife-beater shirt. Director Craig Brewer has said that he wanted there to be 'something both terrifying and titillating' about the poster, where 'you think *Wow, that's wrong and man she looks good and he is all sweaty*'.[84] The movie's sexual frisson comes from the taboo against interracial sex – a taboo which the film treats in a comically exaggerated way but also with some serious emotion: 'I like people to laugh at the outrageousness of it and also be moved,' explains Brewer.[85]

Lazarus says he has Rae on a chain in order to save her from her promiscuity: 'Look, girl, you been runnin' wild on me.' But that 'on me' is troubling. Earlier, we saw Lazarus grab hold of his own wife's hand and try to keep her from running off with another man, warning, 'You better pray, gal.' Does Lazarus want to save or punish Rae, to free her of affliction or to trap her for himself? As Brewer notes, Lazarus has 'pent-up male vengeance inside of him'. He's being 'patient' and 'firm' with Rae like a 'father' to a 'daughter', but 'he's also keeping her captive'.[86] 'Right or wrong,' Lazarus says – as if himself unsure about his motives or the morality of his actions – 'you gonna mind me,' and he pulls Rae towards him with the chain. 'Now we gonna break the hold the devil got on you!' he cries, while we wonder whether *he* is that devil. Previously, Lazarus had sung a blues song about shooting a woman he caught cheating, which was cross-cut with a scene from Rae's past when a man grabbed her from behind and then pulled her to the ground for sex. In the present, when Rae tries to run away, Lazarus grabs her from behind and she screams. Even once she is calm and seated on the couch as Lazarus rubs ointment on her knee wound, his fatherly attention to her threatens to turn into a jilted husband's rage and punitive sexual violence as he speaks to her as if she were his wife 'running around behind my back, whoring!' In these ways, then, Brewer uses pulp luridness to explore some of the emotional complexities of sex and race.

LESBIAN

Mulholland Drive (2001)

Director: David Lynch
Cast: Naomi Watts (Betty/Diane), Laura Harring (Rita/Camilla)

This film features two lesbian love scenes, one a wish-fulfilment fantasy and the other a nightmarish reality. Importantly, though, the fantasy is not purely positive while the nightmare is not entirely negative. The first scene begins with a BFF-bonding moment as Betty cuts Rita's long, brunette hair and gives her a wig so that, as reflected in the bathroom mirror, the two women look like twins with their matching short, blonde hair. The scene has some of the innocent energy of two girls playing dress-up as part of a slumber party sleepover. Soon, a hint of sexuality is introduced as Betty, lying in bed in her pink pyjamas, sees Rita enter wearing nothing but the blonde wig and a crimson bath towel. 'You don't have to wear that in the house,' Betty says, ostensibly referring to the wig, but Rita takes her to mean the towel and, in a way, that is what Betty could have meant. The voluptuous Rita helps bring out the latent meaning, the underlying desire, in girlishly innocent Betty's words. When Betty follows up with 'you don't have to sleep on that couch', the invitation to join her in bed has already become about something more than just getting a 'good night's sleep', even if Betty herself doesn't quite seem to realise it yet. As Rita removes her wig and strips off her towel, revealing her dark hair and curvaceous nude body as she slips into bed, Betty can't help but sneak peeks at her sultry friend, who is now demonstrably more woman than girl. Rita's bare breasts are visible as she leans over just to give Betty a goodnight kiss on the forehead, but Betty tilts her face up with a sigh and kisses Rita on the mouth, first lightly and then with growing passion. Rita takes down Betty's pyjama top and begins to stroke her breasts, helping Betty to discover her own sexuality by seeing and being touched by her friend's female body. Thus Betty's transition from girl to woman is eased by someone *different from* but *still like* her, sensual and yet a girl friend, in a scene that is 'erotic and yet sweet and innocent', as Laura Harring (who plays Rita) describes it.[87]

After they make love, we see Rita lying on her side in the background, her face turned towards Betty's, while Betty is lying face-up in the foreground. The way the shot is framed, their two faces seem to 'meet' at the lips, being joined together to form one composite face. In their love, the two are a perfect fit, each completing the other – friend and lover, innocent and sensual, girlish and womanly. And yet there is also a disturbing sense of narcissism in this too-perfect complementarity. Are lovers really twins, two halves of one whole? Can the other really respond to the self's every desire? It is as if Betty were *in love with herself* in this scene, fantasising a lover whose wishes always coincide with Betty's own, a perfect partner whose *lack of difference from Betty* means that that person could never be real – and if she were real, she would feel oppressed by Betty's overbearing desire.

In fact, this is the nightmare reality we get when Betty and Rita are revealed to be Diane and Camilla, who enact a second sex scene which is the reverse of the first. Rather than meeting Betty/Diane's every desire, Rita/Camilla has been sleeping around with others. As Camilla lies topless and sprawled on a couch – her sexuality all too open and available – Diane straddles her as if to keep her from straying. Jealous and angry, Diane is clad only in the cut-off jeans of a tough girl, her blonde hair dirty and stringy as she has let herself go due to unrequited love. Diane strokes Camilla's breast tenderly, but when her lover says they should break up, Diane works her hand roughly between Camilla's legs, desperately trying to grab hold of her, to re-ignite the passion that once kept them together. After Camilla pushes her away and leaves, Diane is seen masturbating herself roughly on that same couch, presumably fantasising about Camilla. Diane's attempt to possess Camilla, to make the other woman conform to Diane's desires, is thus revealed to have been in part a form of masturbation or self-love, a narcissistic effort to find fulfilment for herself without regard for her friend's autonomous wishes or needs. And yet Diane's self-abuse, her violent masturbation, is more than just an expression of the jealous rage she feels towards Camilla, which she is taking out on herself. It also suggests self-punishment, a realisation on Diane's part that she has ended up alone because of her own narcissistic disregard for Camilla. Moreover, the masturbation implies a deep longing for Camilla to return, a 'reaching for her, reaching in a desperate way to get back to a place where [they] were at before', as Naomi Watts (who plays Diane) explains.[88] Having learned a hard lesson, Diane could finally be reaching beyond narcissism and for real love.

The Gymnast (2006)

Director: Ned Farr
Cast: Dreya Weber (Jane), David De Simone (David), Stef Tovar (Dan), Addie Yungmee (Serena)

Jane is married to David. In order for them to have sex, she turns the football game off and replaces it with softcore porn, then dresses in a 'sexy' bra and panties. Feeling neglected in that she must conform to what her husband desires (or what society has made him think he desires), Jane begins to gravitate towards neighbour and jogging partner Dan. He at least expresses concern about her feelings, but the fact that she easily outruns him is one sign that they are not a good match physically. Jane – a former gymnast whose potential Olympic career was cut short due to injury – has kept in shape by working as a masseuse. Now, under the guidance of an adult gymnastics coach, she in a sense continues that career, practising a Cirque du Soleil-style aerial act with a dancer named Serena. As their coach notes, Serena has 'the grace' while Jane has 'the strength': 'If I can just get the two of you to rub off on each other, then you'll have the whole package.' Practising the act brings the two women together physically and emotionally. In a move called 'porting', Serena hangs suspended from Jane's hands ('I so have you'), then they slowly change places – passing through a 69 position – until Jane is held in Serena's secure grip. In another manoeuvre, the women spread their legs to do the splits, with Serena sitting up and Jane upside-down below her, both joined at the crotch. The women also sit butt-to-butt in the same fabric hammock, extending their upper bodies outwards like a butterfly emerging from a chrysalis.

The film suggests that the lesbian relationship formed with Serena is the natural development of Jane's own desires, just as her career as an aerialist fulfils the promise of her earlier athleticism. Lesbianism is not just an immature phase that she outgrows on the way to heterosexuality, which is how Jane had dismissed the sex she had in college with a former gymnastics team-mate. But nor is 'lesbian' necessarily the identity that Jane claims for herself. Asked whether she thought Serena was straight or gay, Jane says, 'I just thought you were beautiful,' and, after the two have made love, Jane muses, 'I don't feel different. I don't feel "gay" – whatever that means.' (Dreya Weber, the actress who plays Jane, has described herself as 'omnisexual', refusing even to be called 'bisexual' because of the assumptions that can come with that label.)[89] It is patriarchal society that attaches labels. As Jane's husband says, seeing her situation entirely from his perspective (or rather from that of the society he knows will judge him): 'A man turns his wife gay? I'd rather you put a bullet in my head.' When she asks him not to 'put a label on it', his reply is that 'I don't have to. Everybody else will.'

Stereotyping can extend to lesbians themselves, who may be expected to fit the 'butch' or 'femme' model. One reviewer wrote that, while the actress playing Serena looks 'indisputably feminine', Weber (playing Jane) fails to convince: 'Weber's overly developed upper body is at times a distraction. When she dresses up and dons cosmetics to attend an event, she looks like a beefy dyke in formalwear and make-up, not a prettied-up straight former athlete.'[90] But the movie itself strives to break through this butch/femme labelling along with the straight/gay stereotyping. Whereas gymnast Jane may seem to be the 'strength' of the act and dancer Serena its 'grace', Jane wears a soft pink blouse and lipstick when they go out on a date, while Serena is in a rough dark jacket and carries a switchblade knife. Who is butch and who is femme? Jane's softly seductive approach is disarming and Serena lets down her defences, giving Jane her knife. Serena then feels it clipped to Jane's pants when they hug and asks, 'Is that a knife in your pocket or are you just happy to see me?' Which one has the phallus? They both do – because neither does.

Black Swan (2010)

Director: Darren Aronofsky
Cast: Natalie Portman (Nina), Mila Kunis (Lily), Barbara Hershey (Nina's mother)

Nina is a ballerina chosen to dance the lead in *Swan Lake*. While adept at performing the part of the pure and innocent White Swan, she finds herself struggling to embody the passionate Black Swan, a role which the seductive and sensual understudy Lily seems better suited to play. One night Nina slips away from the overprotective and infantilising influence of her mother to go out clubbing with Lily, grinding with her on the dance floor while rolling on Ecstasy. In the back seat of the taxi as they ride home, Lily walks her hand across the distance separating their bodies and pokes Nina's leg, awakening her physical responses. Lily then moves her hand inside Nina's pants, bringing out shudders and sighs from her. However, Nina's hand then acts like her mother's, pulling Lily's hand out and moving it away, preserving Nina's own childlike 'virginity'. But Nina still holds Lily's hand in hers, their fingers interlaced, as though still desirous yet fearful of physical contact.

Back at her mother's apartment, the two amorous young women take a stand against the mother's repressiveness, with Nina seeming to draw on her friend's defiant courage. In one shot, Nina and Lily are reflected in two mirrors whose join makes it look as if they are one body, and the two speak in unison in the face of the disapproving mother, who wants to shut them up. As Nina bars her bedroom door, trying to make a place for herself inside her mother's apartment ('It's called privacy – I'm not twelve any more!'), Lily peeks out from behind Nina's shoulder as though leagued with her, backing her up in her attempt to demarcate a sensual space. Nina intersects with or 'meets' Lily's mirror reflection as she goes to kiss her friend, for in making love with her, Nina is getting in touch with her own sexuality. 'You will have a sex scene with yourself,'[91] as director Darren Aronofsky told Natalie Portman, who plays Nina. Like one woman stripping before a mirror, Lily helps Nina pull off her top and then takes down her pants, after which Nina helps Lily pull off her top and then takes down her pants. In black bra and panties, Lily leans over Nina who is lying back in bed. The seductive Lily feels up Nina's breasts through her white bra, exciting the flesh under the 'pure' exterior. Lily then peels off Nina's white panties, licking between her legs. Like the earlier fingering, this tongue penetration moves inside in order to bring something out. The encounter with this other woman puts Nina in touch with another side of herself, the Black Swan inside the White, the sensual adult within the virginal girl. Sex turns Nina inside-out, allowing her long-repressed desires to surface in the same way that she imagines black wings springing from the tattooed lilies on Lily's back, which undulates as she gives cunnilingus to Nina.

But when Lily looks up from her licking, Nina imagines her own face, like her mother's, *displacing* Lily's and about to berate Nina for being so naughty. Luckily, Lily's face returns to shush the mother's repression by covering Nina's mouth with a kiss. However, after Nina comes – her orgasmic cries having been brought out by Lily's tongue, Nina hears her mother's voice coming from Lily's mouth. For a moment, the words – 'sweet girl' – almost seem to mean the mother's approval of her daughter's sexuality, the sense in which her 'girl' can now fulfil her own grown desires and still be 'sweet'. But then Nina's fear of her mother's stifling protectiveness gets the better of her, as indicated when Nina's own face – so like her mother's – replaces Lily's again, and Nina brings a pink pillow down over her own head, smothering herself.

MARRIAGE

Don't Look Now (1973)

Director: Nicolas Roeg
Cast: Donald Sutherland (John), Julie Christie (Laura)

On vacation in Venice, John and Laura make love in a hotel. Rather than two teens losing their virginity or a pair of lovers committing adultery, this is marital sex. As director Nicolas Roeg says, 'It's not a seduction scene and I think it shocked because it's between a married couple, a natural thing about human urges and needs.'[92] Many details indicate that the sex between this husband and wife is a part of their daily existence, neither hesitantly new nor wildly tempestuous. In the bathroom beforehand, she notices the fat fold around his waist and he sees her plucking breast hairs. And yet the easy intimacy they have with each other's bodies slides naturally over to closeness in bed, as she tells him he has toothpaste on his mouth and he leans over, asking her to 'eat it off'. The bedroom scene is conjugally real, not prettied up in the way it might be for newlyweds. There is a spot of wetness visible on her neck from one of his kisses, and we see that he is still wearing socks during part of the act. Later, she licks his bare foot and his armpit – presumably because this is what they like to do, even though these moves hardly belong to the standard repertoire of movie sex scenes. She even strokes his bare buttock, without their seeming to fear that this will somehow make him look passive or lacking in masculinity. She is also neither shy nor aggressive about getting what she wants. Opening her nightgown, she puts his hand on her breast and has him go down on her, which he comfortably does as he has clearly done it before. Throughout the scene, shots of the couple making love are cross-cut with shots of them dressing for dinner afterwards, suggesting that their sex is continuous with the rest of their life together, the 'now' a natural part of later (dinner) and before (the bathroom), their lovemaking only one element in the extended physical and emotional intimacy that is their marriage.

But this cross-cutting also adds a poignancy to the scene, implying that theirs is a fleeting connection, their time together shot through with the sense that they will soon be apart. A shot of Laura opening her nightgown for him to reach her breasts is followed by another of her putting on her blouse for dinner. A shot of David naked and thrusting on top of her is cross-cut with one of him zipping up his trousers. Their timeless moment of ecstasy is also a moment in time, as indicated by the watch visible on his arm throughout and by the clock on the nightstand which he will later consult to reset his watch to the correct time. As Roeg says, the scene 'does have a great sadness to it, as well as happiness or pleasure'[93] – the sadness of imminent parting which imbues every moment together. And yet their brief convergence also carries over and on through their time apart. The emotional connection between them lingers as an after-effect of their physical contact, as suggested by the cut from their kissing to her licking her lips in front of the mirror afterwards, or by the cut from his hand on her naked back during lovemaking to his hand on her clothed back as they walk out to dinner. Their connection may carry on in another sense, too: Roeg has said that 'at the moment of making love she might have become pregnant'.[94]

Bliss (1997)

Director: Lance Young
Cast: Sheryl Lee (Maria), Craig Sheffer (Joseph), Terence Stamp (sex therapist Baltazar)

After six months of marriage, Maria suddenly reveals to Joseph in a therapy session, 'I have a confession to make: I fake my orgasms.' This admission is cross-cut with shots of him making love to her in the marital bed as she writhes in the ecstasy of climax – only now he realises that this image of them as a happy couple has been a mere façade: 'You're a lie. Our whole marriage is a lie.' In another scene, she surreptitiously unzips and masturbates him in a semi-public place. When he says, 'Honey, that's enough,' she replies, 'Oh, we'll both know when it's enough, darling.' While his orgasm is visible in ejaculation, hers is not. How can he *know* when hers is real? Seeing a sex therapist, Joseph is eventually able to give a detailed description of how he feels when making love to his wife, but when asked 'How does *she* feel?' he can only answer, 'I don't know.' But learning about himself is the first step. Taking the therapist's advice, Joseph first shows Maria how he likes to be touched before asking her to demonstrate on herself. As she realises, 'He wanted to know how to please me.' The therapist also advises Joseph not to fixate on orgasm as proof of love but instead to use his 'ring finger' on her 'yoni' (vagina) to find the 'sacred spot' (G-spot): 'All of Maria's abuse and psychic hurts reside in this sacred spot. It will take time to release them.' Combining elements of western sexology and tantric sexuality, this therapy redefines a true husband not as someone who finds proof of his own prowess in his wife's orgasm, but as someone who cares enough to know how she feels and whose love can heal her body and soul.

Initially, what Maria feels is anger at the father who sexually abused her when she was a child – and shame over her body's unwanted physiological response of pleasure mixed in with the pain. Tying Joseph's hands and feet to the bed frame so that he is rendered passive in the way that she felt as a child, Maria gets on top of him, bites his body aggressively and then rides him until he orgasms against his will, while she says, 'I love you so deep inside me.' Joseph is both the stand-in for herself as a child and a man like her father against whom she takes revenge. Maria is now the one in control, but she is also out of control, the abused become the abuser, repeating the violence which she inflicts on her surrogate self and once again confusing pain with pleasure. Yet it is Joseph's love for her that has allowed her to open up, to abuse him on the way to her own healing. 'Acting out her abuse fantasy is what enables Maria to get past the guilt and anxiety of being intimate,' the therapist says. In the film's final scene, Joseph and Maria are curled up naked in bed together. Regardless of whether they are having sex, he *knows* that they are making love.

A History of Violence (2005)

Director: David Cronenberg
Cast: Viggo Mortensen (Tom), Maria Bello (Edie)

Small-town Indiana. Tom and Edie have been married for ten years and there are two significant sex scenes between them in the film. In the first, as director David Cronenberg describes it, 'they're playing cheerleader and high-school jock'.[95] Edie enters the bedroom wearing a cheerleader's outfit, lifting her skirt to flash her panties, then removes Tom's belt with one pull, takes down his trousers and pushes him back onto the bed. 'What have you done with my wife?' Tom wonders, while Edie leaps onto him, saying

'Go, Wildcats! No wives in here, mister.' If he thinks she's 'naughty', she tells him he's 'such a bad boy' when he strips off her panties, twirls them above his head and then plunges his face between her legs. In this scene, Tom and Edie take on excitingly other identities: the all-American 'good girl' cheerleader who nevertheless exposes herself and is hungry for sex, the domesticated husband who becomes a wild man in the bedroom. But, in adopting these other identities, Tom and Edie never lose sight of who they are. This is *role-play* that they know as such, an edgily erotic scenario built on the secure foundation of their marriage. Even during sex with the 'wildcat', he knows that the wife will return, and she that the husband is still there in the 'bad boy'. In fact, as Tom goes down on her, Edie notes that 'there wasn't much of *that* in high school'. The considerateness of the husband *shows through* the 'bad boy', for if Tom were truly a tough-guy jock, he would take his own pleasure and not give her cunnilingus. Similarly, if all she wanted was to get off, Edie would not then manoeuvre herself into a 69 position – as she does – in order to offer him satisfaction, too.

The second sex scene occurs after Edie has found out about Tom's past life as a big-city gangster and vicious killer named Joey. When Edie tries to flee from him by running up the staircase in their house, Tom grabs her by the neck and holds her pinned against the wall. 'Fuck you, Joey!' she says, naming the thug in him. He wrestles her down onto the stairs, lying on top of her and gripping her neck with his hand, but then he begins to turn away, seeming to have second thoughts about what he is doing. She, however, grabs his head and pulls his face towards hers for a kiss, which is then followed by rough sex that they both have right there, bruising themselves on the wooden stairs and almost falling down them. She cries out as she comes from his violent thrusts. Afterwards, as she kisses and embraces him, we can see the wedding ring on her hand that she has balled into a fist held behind his head. She looks at him in disgust and then flees upstairs, leaving him alone at the bottom. Here, as in the first sex scene, Tom and Edie take on other identities, but this time there is no longer a secure foundation for their role-play. This time, when they lose themselves, it's not clear whether they will ever find themselves again. One reason Edie has sex in this scene is that 'she's still looking for the Tom that's in this creature' Joey, says Cronenberg.[96] She wants to find the husband in the bad boy, to bring him out with her love. That one moment where this thug turns away, seemingly willing to let her go, is enough for Edie to pull him to her, as if she could pull Tom out of Joey, attract her husband back to her. But there could also be a second reason: 'Maybe there's even something about Joey that is exciting, that is exhilarating. ...There's a great intense sexuality that comes out of this situation, and a desperation and at this moment also a disgust, a revulsion, not only in terms of what Tom has done to their lives but in terms of what she's just done, the fact that she fucked this guy that she barely knows and it's been satisfying and that scares her.'[97] As married couples do, Edie has defined herself in relation to Tom, but if he is no longer a husband, is she a wife? As Edie loses her grip on who Tom is, the bottom drops out of her own identity. If she's attracted to a violent man, does that mean she enjoys being violated? The first sex scene allowed the couple to go out of themselves only to find their identities secured again in the end. This time Edie fears that, in having sex with a stranger, she has become a stranger to herself.

NAZIS

The Night Porter (1974)

Director: Liliana Cavani
Cast: Dirk Bogarde (Max), Charlotte Rampling (Lucia)

World War Two. Max is an SS officer at a concentration camp where Lucia is imprisoned. Max films the naked inductees, singling

Lucia out with the camera's spotlight. Like all the others, she is exposed and vulnerable in her enforced nudity – even more so, given the camera's eye – but she also receives special attention as the particular object of his gaze. Later, the inmates and Lucia watch while a guard sodomises a male prisoner, who appears to be masturbating himself during the act. The sight is confusing: given the power imbalance and the virtual impossibility of saying no, this is evidently a rape, yet the prisoner seems to be taking pleasure from the act. He is being particularly victimised but at the same time singled out for special attention. After watching this encounter, Lucia is led by Max into another room where 'he chained Lucia to the bed so he could better caress her' and 'he had her arm subjected to torture so that he could kiss her wounds gently', as director Liliana Cavani describes it.[98] The chains and the caress, the torture and the tenderness, are confusing because Lucia feels pleasure right after pain, sensuality very close to brutality, and in this way she comes to have a masochistic response to Max's domineering 'love'. According to Cavani, 'Their strange relationship was a combination of profound tenderness and cruelty. ...She seemed to respond to these experiences without aversion, sometimes even with satisfaction'.[99]

Later, Lucia performs a strange dance for Max and some other Nazis. Wearing an SS cap and a man's suspenders and trousers, Lucia rubs her own black-gloved hands over her bare breasts as she leans against a post. It is as though she were re-enacting the scene where Max chained her to a bedpost and caressed her breasts, only this time she is *both Max and herself*, both the Nazi and the sexualised victim. Thus her body enacts the confusion in her mind, the sense in which she has internalised her oppressor, has come to 'love' the abuse. Continuing her dance, Lucia puts one arm behind her head and the other down her trousers, like the prisoner she saw masturbating while being held and taken from behind by a Nazi guard. Now she has become that prisoner, finding her own pleasure in the pain being inflicted upon her. Rather than simply suffering as another anonymous victim, she perversely 'enjoys' being in the spotlight, singled out for their attention as she dances, enacting with her body the sado-masochistic scenario they desire. And when, as a special reward for her dance, Max brings her the severed head of a fellow inmate who had been bullying her, Lucia gets another terrible kind of 'enjoyment'. Now she – who had only wanted the inmate transferred – can feel complicit in the killing of others, as if she really were a Nazi and not what she in fact is: someone severely traumatised and sexually disturbed by what they have done to her.

Salò, or The 120 Days of Sodom (Salò, o le 120 giornate di Sodoma) (1975)

Director: Pier Paolo Pasolini
Cast: Sergio Fascetti (Sergio), Renata Moar (Renata), Giorgio Cataldi (the bishop)

Near the end of World War Two, four Italian fascists sexually abuse, torture and kill a number of young men and women. In a way that suggests internalised homophobia, gay director Pier Paolo Pasolini has picked up some unfortunate elements from his source text, The 120 Days of Sodom (1785), written by the Marquis de Sade. As in Sade, the film associates homosexuality and anal intercourse with pain, shit and death. By contrast, heterosexuality is depicted as a positive alternative and linked to life-affirming pleasure and procreation. Following a marriage ceremony in which two of the young people, Sergio and Renata, exchange sacred vows, the fascists strip them of their wedding attire and order them down on the ground to copulate like animals. However, Sergio strokes Renata's face with tenderness and she affectionately ruffles his hair. They kiss with the shyness of newlyweds and embrace with true feeling for each other, only then lying down and moving towards making love. But this is too much humanity for their cruel masters to countenance. The fascists separate the couple and, asserting the lord and master's 'right to the first night' ('This flower is reserved for us!'), they forcibly sodomise the newlyweds, taking pleasure in their pain, consolidating power through their punishment. Each fascist likes to think of himself as 'tall and endowed with an enormous member. He is also extremely rich, very powerful, severe and cruel – with a heart of stone.' It is as though having a 'heart of stone' gets him hard. His phallus is a weapon that, by inflicting pain, allows him to get off on his sense of power. The young men and women – 'these innocent children' – are there only to be defiled, empowering their perverse masters by allowing themselves to be reduced to 'weak, chained creatures, destined for our pleasure'.

Does the film then become, like Sade's text, a 'brutally dehumanising kind of pornography that annihilates the human person, reducing it to a disposable pleasure machine'?[100] Not quite. Consider the relationship between one of the fascists – a bishop – and an anonymous young man known only as a 'fucker' and chosen for the size of his cock. When the 'fucker' sodomises the bishop, this blasphemous act may seem typical of the 'anal defilement' often engaged in by the fascists, as when they buggered the newlyweds. One difference, though, is that here the fascist is on the receiving end; it is not he who is getting a hard-on from committing cruelty. More importantly, this is anal sex that does not appear to involve pain and that both men seem to enjoy. The young man smiles and pants in excitement as he rides the moaning bishop's back, thrusting so vigorously that the two fall from the bed to the floor where, after some more energetic coupling, they orgasm. Following this, they lie entwined for a while before rising to their knees, when the young man pulls the smiling bishop to him for a passionate and extended kiss. Would they linger like this if the sex had been dolorous and degrading? Here, at least, the fascist and the 'fucker' seem to have become persons again, humanised through shared bodily pleasure.

The Reader (2008)

Director: Stephen Daldry
Cast: David Kross (Young Michael), Kate Winslet (Hanna), Vijessna Ferkic (Sophie), Ralph Fiennes (Adult Michael)

West Germany 1958. 15-year-old Michael has a summer-long love affair with an older woman, Hanna, who is 36. Their first contact occurs when he falls ill with scarlet fever in her entryway. She wipes vomit from his mouth and hugs away his sobs, providing him with the physical and emotional comfort that a mother would. Visiting her some days later, he sees her ironing her bra and fastening her stockings to her garter belt, much as a son might catch a glimpse of his mother's underclothes. When he is covered in coal dust after performing a household chore for her, she has him strip and take a bath where, as boys will, he gets an erection. To hide it, he stands with his back to her as she towels him off, but then she drops the towel, revealing that she, too, is naked, and reaches around to masturbate him. In this way, Hanna moves almost imperceptibly from mother to lover, revealing sexuality to him, bathing and 'birthing' him into manhood. When Michael gets between her spread legs and enters her, he asks if he is doing it right and she reassures him, putting her hands behind him to guide his gentle thrusts. As a result of her sexual solicitude, Michael is able to complete his masculine rite of passage, gaining 'a knowingness, a swagger' and 'a terrific physical confidence' in all aspects of his life.[101] While on a cycling holiday with Hanna, Michael kisses her in front of a waitress who has mistaken her for his mother, as if to prove that he is grown up enough to have an older woman like Hanna for his own. Naturally, Michael wants to try out his new-found confidence and sophistication on a girl his own age, the virginal Sophie, to whom he finds himself attracted. Sensing this, Hanna makes passionate love with him one more time, then releases him to join other teenagers, disappearing from his life for good. Although he is devastated by her loss, feeling that his lover has forsaken him, there is a sense in which her job as a 'mother' is done: she has helped him to grow up, and even the breaking of his heart can be seen as part of that.

What Michael did not know during the affair – what he finds out only years later – is that Hanna had two secrets: she was illiterate and she had once served as a guard in a concentration camp. These two realisations on the part of the adult Michael put the relationship he had had with her in a different light, allowing him to see things – for the first time – from *her* perspective. Now he understands why Hanna was so suspicious when he first asked her name – she thought he might be after her for her crimes – and why she made love with such passionate abandon, as if she could somehow lose herself in sex: her 'seductiveness... was an invitation to forget the world in the recesses of the body'; 'we made love as if nothing else in the world mattered'.[102] But he also sees why she had him read aloud to her before sex, how she had wanted him to help her open up and connect physically and emotionally with the world around her. In one remembered lovemaking scene, for example, Michael was moving inside Hanna while we heard a voice-over of him reading, 'I poked into the place a ways, encountered a little open patch.' In their last time together, Hanna gave naked Michael a full-body scrub, perhaps repeating and attempting to atone for what she had done to the concentration camp inmates, loving the bodies that had been lost and trying to clean her conscience. Then, Michael recalls, 'we made love' and 'I sensed that she wanted to push me to the point of feeling things I had never felt before, to the point where I could no longer stand it. She also gave herself in a way she had never done before.'[103] Without realising it at the time, Michael had helped her to connect with love and loss, to feel – through her love for him – the pain of what she had done to the inmates. In the end, she loved him enough to free him – from herself.

PROSTITUTION

The Centre of the World (2001)

Director: Wayne Wang
Cast: Peter Sarsgaard (Richard), Molly Parker (Florence)

Richard is a dot.com entrepreneur who pays a stripper named Florence to join him on a trip to Las Vegas. Because she does not want to feel like a prostitute, Florence sets certain rules for their erotic play: 'No talk about feelings, no kissing on the mouth, no penetration... no fucking.' These conditions imply that there is a connection between interfacial intimacy and genital intercourse, between true feelings and actual fucking. Florence is willing to engage in other sexual practices for pay, but penetration – like kissing – is sensual *and* emotional; it is sexual in a way that involves her core self, which is something she won't sell. However, as she and Richard spend time together, Florence begins to know and like him as a person. He is lonely – like her – and seems genuinely nice to her. In return, she is increasingly tempted to do more for him than she would for other clients, as when she fulfils his secret 'fire and ice' fantasy involving ice cubes and warm liquor on his anus. On the one hand, this act shows her satisfying the desire of her customer and conforming to *his* fantasy. On the other hand, this particular fantasy reveals a certain vulnerability in Richard and a potential willingness to open up that is unusual in a man and which she finds touching. As actor Peter Sarsgaard (Richard) notes, 'For a heterosexual man, the biggest taboo has to be his asshole,'[104] and Richard allows his to be penetrated – by Florence. Also, Florence sees Richard realise the discrepancy between porn scenario and fleshly fact when his 'fire and ice' fantasy ends up being more than a little painful in reality and he has to ask her to stop: 'this guy's ultimate sexual fantasy' turns out to 'ultimately kind of suck'.[105] When Florence breaks her own rules and allows Richard to kiss her and penetrate her, it is because his opening himself up to her has led her to feel for him as a person and to want to reveal her core self to him.

The struggle within Richard's mind between porn fantasy and interpersonal reality can be seen in the different meanings given to the film's title. Richard begins by believing that, as a computer engineer sitting in front of his monitor all day, 'you're kind of connected to everybody and everything. It's like you're at the centre of the world.' But Florence tries to get him to see that 'woman's cunt' is 'the centre of the world', that her flesh is not his fantasy – he needs to *know* her if they are ever going to have a real connection. Richard is used to buying sex online in the form of cyber-porn females who will perform to order: 'The dot-commer is really trying to treat [sex] like an object in a computer and try to manipulate it, because that's how they think – they think they're the master of the universe,' says director Wayne Wang.[106] In fact, the website used to promote this movie encouraged visitors to satisfy their desires by making a stripper strip and by ordering up a virtual lap dance, which is what Richard first did in 'real life' when he 'interacted' with Florence at a strip club.

Now the question is whether Richard can move from fantasist to realist, from master to lover. Moaning and jerking off in front of his computer, Richard watches a virtual stripper peel off her black lace panties and say with her red lips, 'I want you inside me – please!' Her image is programmed to meet his desires, but note that what he wants is for *her* to want him, to find him desirable and to let him in. 'Tell me you want me inside of you so bad,' Richard says to himself, dictating what she should say. But at the same time, is he trying to make contact through words, to encourage her to like him, to feel himself worthy of being wanted? As he speaks, Richard is filmed in grainy digital video. Perhaps this is all just his porn fantasy, but it could be that he has entered the virtual world in an attempt to meet her on her own ground, to interact with her and pull her out into the real world with him. 'I just pull you onto me, and your whole body just shakes,' he says, imagining that *she* responds to him, is moved to her core by his desire, 'and you feel like you're gonna come, and you feel like I'm gonna come' – as though the desire and the satisfaction were both mutual. When Florence does finally allow Richard to penetrate her and the two moan while engaged in actual intercourse, is it the fulfilment of Richard's truest desire, which is real and reciprocal enjoyment? 'Oh, God, I'm gonna come inside you,' he says. 'I love you.' Or has he merely projected his own virtual desires onto the real-world Florence, selfishly and pathetically imagining that she – someone he is paying and whom he doesn't even really know – desires and climaxes with him?

RELIGION

The Devil's Playground (1976)

Director: Fred Schepisi
Cast: Simon Burke (Tom), Arthur Dignam (Francine), John Diedrich (Fitz), Alan Cinis (Waite), Michael David (Turner), Thomas Keneally (Marshall), Nick Tate (Victor)

Rural Australia 1953. Thirteen-year-old Tom receives a repressive religious education at a seminary for boys. In a place where nothing is permitted, everything becomes eroticised. When Brother Francine discovers that Tom has slipped off his swim trunks and is showering nude, the monk admonishes the boy to 'be on your guard against all your senses' because 'your body is your worst enemy'. Whether or not Tom's explanation that he was merely trying to get completely clean is true, he will certainly be more sensually aware – and more guiltily lascivious – after the Brother's tongue-lashing. Beyond swimming and showering, the connection between water imagery and sexuality continues when we find that Tom is troubled by two kinds of nocturnal emissions: wet dreams and bed-wetting. Ironically (considering water's irrepressible flow), a priest gives Tom some holy water from Lourdes to help cure the latter problem. Making the connection between 'wetting the bed' and 'whacking off', Tom's friend Fitz mockingly recommends that Tom apply the Lourdes water to his 'dick' rather than his tongue in order to 'stop all the pissing and the pulling'. Tom is peeling carrots during this conversation, an act that takes on masturbatory connotations given the boys' lewd talk. In another scene, Fitz instructs Tom – 'Just pull, that's it!' – as they work a giant saw together over a log, the older boy introducing the younger to physical experience related to manhood. Later, after agreeing to 'wrestle' with a younger boy named Waite and then to 'squeeze' each other's dicks, Tom tries to teach him the next step ('Don't you want to be pulled?'), but Waite is afraid to take their erotic play to the point of ejaculation. 'Wrestling' and 'squeezing' aren't really sex; they seem part of a polymorphously perverse sensuality. But once it is localised and manifested in semen, it becomes defined as sex – and thus as sinful in the eyes of an ascetic religion.

One night Tom happens upon a group of boys who are whipping each other's bare backs and emitting cries of ecstasy. As their leader Turner says, 'Welcome to our purification, Tom. Come, bare your despicable body. Let us beat out your evils.' Pain becomes these boys' avenue to pleasure, and purification their excuse for making near-naked bodily contact with one another and reaching a morally acceptable kind of orgasm. Turner's sado-masochistic sexuality ultimately leads to death, as his naked body is found in the freezing lake – a sign that his spirit could not accept the warm waters flowing from, through and around him. Similarly, Brother Francine can only sneak shame-faced peeks at women's bodies around a public pool, and when he later dreams of swimming naked with them, all his sin-obsessed mind can imagine is their hands on his body pulling him down to a death by drowning.

'Forevermore, we shall be awash in the burning rivers of the dead,' preaches Father Marshall in his hellfire sermon against giving way to the temptations of the flesh. But, almost miraculously, Tom remains open to both physical and spiritual love, as in the scene where he masturbates to a magazine image of a woman modelling a brassiere, which is right next to a picture of Christ. Brother Victor notes that Tom has 'constantly got an erection. Talk about sex rearing its ugly head – it just about rears him off the ground permanently.' Perhaps, rather than dragging him down to death, sex will contribute to Tom's spiritual ascension, to his permanent place in heaven.

Behind Convent Walls (Interno di un convento) (1977)

Director: Walerian Borowczyk
Cast: Gabriella Giacobbe (abbess) Ligia Branice (Clara), Howard Ross (Rodrigo)

Early nineteenth-century Italy. The abbess of a convent reminds the sisters that they have 'sworn to be faithful to Christ' and that any form of profane love must be resisted as 'sacrilegious: it is cheating on your spouse with Satan'. However, the abbess's zealous repression of her charges' sinful desires suggests that she herself is finding erotic expression through the very means of her vehement denial. The sword-cane she uses to poke through the nuns' mattresses in search of concealed love letters implies her own desire for penetration. The erotic watercolours she drowns in a basin of water bring her into close visual and tactile proximity to sensual images. When the abbess catches a nun engaging in auto-erotic activity, then insists that the woman repeat her masturbation in front of her and afterwards confiscates the dildo, it is the abbess's own jealous voyeurism and her desire to take secret satisfaction later that are revealed.

As for the nuns, the forbidden nature of their passion seems to fan its flames. When even the touching of eyebrows is prohibited, doing so takes on a sensual charge as one novitiate finds that rubbing them can bring her to orgasm. Another nun is denied the aural pleasures of music in the chapel and so she pushes a violin between her legs while stroking the neck of the instrument. When one sister fondles another's breast as she exposes it through her nun's habit, the fact that their sex-play occurs behind the partially open curtains of a confessional adds the thrill of exhibitionism to the sinful excitements of lesbianism and blasphemy.

This brazen enactment of sin is hardly the kind of confession the church expects from those desiring atonement, but what if sexual expression and not pious repression were the way to God? If 'nunsploitation' films get a sexual charge out of sacrilege, they also gesture towards a utopia where profane love is accepted as sacred, where sex is no longer sinful. As a handyman penetrates a log with his axe, a piece of wood (symbol of his desire) flies up, falling from 'heaven' at the feet of a nun as if in answer to her most fervent prayers. She whittles the wood into a dildo, attaches the image of the man she desires to it and then pleasures herself, using a hand-mirror to watch its movement between her legs. 'Don't you have any shame?' the abbess scolds her, but why is the nun's watching – or our watching – so wrong? Why shouldn't she use what has been providentially given – her eyes, her sex, the wood – for her pleasure? Another nun, Sister Clara, has ecstatic visions of uniting with Christ while her lover Rodrigo has sex with her. 'Penetrate me' and 'come', she says as she experiences her passion. Rather than condemning the physical, she wants love to encompass both body and soul: 'I want to love you with my whole being.' Later, when interrogated about how the man got in, she refuses all blame for letting him 'defile' her, asserting instead that heaven opened the door to her love, which was both natural and holy: 'I spent the night with the man I love, the man who loves me. But I didn't open the door. I found it that way. It was already open.'

SENSUALITY

9 ½ Weeks (1986)

Director: Adrian Lyne
Cast: Mickey Rourke (John), Kim Basinger (Elizabeth)

This film's sex scene involving food from a refrigerator teeters on the brink of absurdity – a fact recognised by the subsequent parodies which pushed it right over. In *Fatal Instinct* (1993), a couple has sex *inside* a refrigerator, causing it to shake vigorously and then spill them out onto the kitchen floor. In *Hot Shots* (1991), a man not only runs an ice cube over a woman's bare belly, but literally fries an egg and two strips of bacon on her sizzling 'hot body'. However, *9½ Weeks* presents its edible eroticism with some seriousness. Michael encourages Elizabeth, who works as an assistant in an art gallery, to expand her senses beyond the visual. He blindfolds her and shakes a glass of ice cubes so that she can hear the watery clink. He runs an ice cube up her chin and tantalises her mouth with it, provoking her thirst. He then runs some ice around her exposed nipple and down her bare midriff, letting some water pool in her belly button, causing her to feel the heat of her body in contrast to the cold. In another scene, Michael has her close her eyes and open up her ears to the sound of an egg being cracked into a bowl – first the sharp tap and then the liquid pour. He then feeds her some maraschino cherries and a cherry tomato so that she can taste the contrast between sweet and acidic, followed by cherry Jell-O and jalapeño peppers with their clash between sweet and spicy, smooth and rough. Liquids he has her drink include fine champagne followed by cheap cough syrup. The milk she imbibes runs down her chin, and Michael spritzes sparkling water from a bottle all over her body, making these liquids tactile as well as a matter of taste. Through it all, Elizabeth tries to sniff out what she is being served.

She bites down greedily or almost spits up, laughing or making a sour face depending on what's put in her mouth. With all her senses so stimulated, it's no wonder that actress Kim Basinger (Elizabeth) has said that 'I was like an exposed nerve throughout the filming'.[107] And all these tastes, smells and textures serve to whet her appetite for love, the sensuous spilling over into the sensual. In the novel, Elizabeth describes feeling 'heat, fear, cold, pleasure, hunger, glut, pain, desire, overwhelming lust. ...My body alive and pliant around me, soon to turn liquid or afire.'[108] Michael drips honey onto her tongue and over her bare legs, rubbing the sticky-sweet substance up her thighs and then consuming her mouth with kisses. The lovemaking that then follows is not shown – and why should it be? Haven't they already had sex?

Lady Chatterley (2006)

Director: Pascale Ferran
Cast: Marina Hands (Constance), Hippolyte Girardot (Clifford), Jean-Louis Coullo'ch (Parkin)

1920s England. Constance is in a sexless marriage to wealthy and domineering Clifford, who is paralysed from the waist down. Increasingly, she seeks escape from the confines of him and his country house by going forth into the surrounding woodlands and into the arms of a gentle gamekeeper, Parkin. Director Pascale Ferran has said that the actress playing Constance had to be 'someone who is very much in touch with the senses and who is able to convey a certain sensuality'.[109] Gradually, the pale-skinned and heavily clothed Constance opens herself up to the natural world around her and to Parkin's body. Walking through the woods, she delights in the blooming daffodils. Later, she and Parkin run naked through this forest and he puts a tiny daisy between her legs, showing that her sex is as naturally beautiful as a flower. Another time after making love, she sees that his penis is 'tiny now, like a bud', calling attention to its delicacy and potentiality, not just to its hard-thrusting virility. In a different scene, Parkin shows her some birds' nests in a copse and he has her hold a newly hatched pheasant chick in her hand. 'It's so trusting,' she says while stroking it. Later, as we hear the sound of birds in the background, Constance touches his face, running her fingers over his lips, his chin and down his neck. Then she moves her hand up the inside of his thigh to hold his erect cock through his shirt-tails, caressing it. 'All three of us were very prudish,' Ferran says about herself and her two lead players. 'To remove that petrifying fear, we worked through the sex scenes as if they were important dialogue scenes, but with gestures replacing words.'[110]

The couple's increasing intimacy and Constance's sensual awakening are also conveyed through tactile imagery of trees and water. First she drinks from cupped hands near a stream and later works a pump to spill water into her lover's hands. Another time, the two sip from glasses of water while he notices the perspiration running down the side of her face. When she gets caught in a rain shower, her clothes are drenched, and afterwards she strips down with him so that they can both run naked in the downpour. Constance's first sight of Parkin's shirtless back as he is bathing himself so excites her that she has to sit down, panting, in the forest. Later she leans against a tree, feeling its bark, then sits with her back against Parkin's chest as he embraces her from behind. In another scene, he spreads his coat beneath a tree in the woods. While he sits with his back to the trunk, she straddles him and they make love, ending with the two of them lying languorously side by side on the leafy forest floor, looking up at the tree sighing above them. 'We came together this time,' Parkin says, and he might as well be referring to nature as to the two of them.

SEX AND DEATH

Damage (1992)

Director: Louis Malle
Cast: Jeremy Irons (Stephen), Juliette Binoche (Anna), Rupert Graves (Martyn)

Stephen, a highly respected British politician, is having an extramarital affair with Anna, a younger woman who is also engaged to be married to his own son, Martyn. At the climax of *Damage*, Martyn opens an apartment door and discovers his father naked on top of his fiancée, grunting and thrusting while she has her head thrown back, moaning in passion. Stunned, Martyn walks dazedly backwards out the door, tumbles over a banister and falls headlong down a stairwell to a crashing death below. This scene links sex and death in numerous ways. In watching his father in bed with his fiancée, Martyn sees himself displaced, excluded – annihilated in a sense, as if his father had inflicted upon him a crushingly 'terrible blow'.[111] Witnessing the father whom he had idolised engaged in such base behaviour destroys Martyn's image of Stephen and strikes at his own sense of himself as his father's son, crumpling his self-image.

From Stephen's perspective, sex with Anna brings on his own demise in several senses. His climax with her leads to the end of his life as he has known it, for when the affair is exposed following his son's death, Stephen loses his identity as a revered politician, an adored husband and a proud father. By claiming his son's fiancée, Stephen was in sexual competition with Martyn, not wanting to be displaced by a younger, more virile man: 'I realised that my son... had become at last and most dangerously my rival. ...He's your match in bed. ...Bed, bed, with Anna.'[112] Ironically, in trying to prove his greater potency, Stephen ends up destroying his own lineage by killing the son in whom the father would have lived on through future generations. All that vigorous thrusting on Stephen's part leads to impotence, as shown when he leaves Anna's bed and runs naked down the stairs, his limp penis flapping, in a futile attempt to save Martyn, who already lies dead on the floor. By selfishly hoarding all the women – his own wife and his son's fiancée – this father ends up with nothing, for both Anna and his wife leave him.

Even before the fatal climax, Stephen had sensed the doom towards which his desire was tending: 'I knew I was on a headlong rush to destruction'[113] – headlong like the plunge that Martyn would take after seeing Stephen with Anna. In an earlier sex scene, Anna is lying back with her arms spread out – like 'Christ... nailed to the cross' – as Stephen penetrates her, as if instead of making love, her body were being sacrificed to his lust: 'I forced all parts of her to feed my need... Patiently, she suffered the slow torments of my adoration.'[114] In another scene emphasising the selfish and self-destructive violence of his desire, he tears off her top and plunges his face between her breasts, causing them both to fall backwards off a chair. As he fucks her on the floor, he bangs her head against it (as Martyn will soon hit his head when he falls). It's as though Stephen is making Anna suffer for his desire, which he knows is wrong and must be punished, should be stopped – before it is too late. On that deadly day in the apartment, Stephen and Anna are both reflected in mirrors. Then they sit facing each other and entwined, their similar short, dark hair making them look like one body doubled in a mirror – the egotistical Stephen in love with himself, heedless of the pain he causes Anna or of the shock that will kill his son. Though it may seem the ultimate in fulfilment, Stephen's narcissistic sex destroys all others and is regressive to the point of self-annihilation.

The Living End (1992)

Director: Gregg Araki
Cast: Craig Gilmore (Jon), Mike Dytri (Luke)

Jon and Luke are both HIV-positive. Despite a doctor's advice that they shouldn't 'consider this a death sentence', Luke plans to 'just off myself' if he sees the 'first symptom' of AIDS on his body rather than suffer through the disease and endure a slow death. Wearing tight jeans, a muscle T-shirt and a leather jacket, Luke follows the rebel's credo: 'Live fast, die young and leave a beautiful corpse.' While Luke's HIV status has given him an increased lust for life ('we gotta grab life by the balls and go for it'), it also seems to have instilled in him a desire for an early death, with *thanatos* overshadowing *eros* more and more in his relationship with Jon. While Jon is driving, Luke wants him to reach over and feel Luke's boner, and later he gives Jon head under the steering wheel while their car passes police on the side of the road. When does flouting the law, defiantly having sex in the face of death, become a provocation to arrest, a drive towards destruction? In a motel shower, Luke wants Jon inside him even though his lover doesn't have a condom. When Luke says 'I don't care', it is a sign of the strength of his love that he would value Jon above his own life, but it is also a despairing indifference to life and an active flirtation with death. 'When I start to come, choke me,' Luke says, and later he wonders if 'death is a lot like coming' since the 'same chemicals and stuff get released in the bloodstream'. Luke is trying to overcome his fear of death by seeing it as synonymous with the pleasure of orgasm, by confusing death with 'the little death' of sexual climax.

In the process, though, he further endangers not only his own life but also that of his lover. The fellatio while driving and the unprotected sex in the shower make Jon a party to Luke's self-destruction and in the worst way – being sucked into risky behaviour and into possibly killing his partner Luke by making love to him. No wonder Jon tells Luke that 'I have this vision of you as a vampire, sucking the life force out of me'. What should be mutually sustaining sex has become a death pact that Jon feels seduced into signing. Luke strokes around Jon's mouth with a gun as if expecting him to suck it, but when he won't, Luke pistol-whips him and then licks the blood off Jon's face. Here loving care is undercut by a desire to consume, as Luke's wish to cure Jon gives way to a despairing urge to unite their contaminated blood in death. In the film's last scene, Luke puts the gun to his own head while having forcible sex with Jon, who tearfully tells him, 'What the fuck are you waiting for? Just do it! Do it!' Although Jon's tears protest and mourn the act, he loves Luke so much that he is willing to help him achieve the orgasmic death he desires, willing even to join Luke in a climactic suicide pact. Luke pulls the trigger as he comes, but the gun is out of bullets. The film leaves Luke having to face something harder to do than dying: living and loving with HIV.

Kissed (1996)

Director: Lynne Stopkewich
Cast: Molly Parker (Sandra), Peter Outerbridge (Matt)

Sandra works as an embalmer at a funeral home where she makes love to the corpses of young men. But when she meets Matt, she is torn between her necrophilia and the possibility of an intimate relationship with a living boyfriend. Sandra has confused sex and death from the time that she was a girl when she misunderstood her first menstrual flow, thinking that it was blood from a dead animal which she had been rubbing over her body. Now, when she is erotically attracted to a cadaver in the embalming room, she dances naked around him then straddles his head so that blood from his mouth will stimulate her sex. Matt tries to get Sandra to dance with him in his apartment, but she declines, saying that she is not very good at it. When they kiss, it is painfully awkward. Sensing her distress and knowing the kind of contact Sandra prefers, Matt has her lie back so that he can give her head, but she remains unresponsive. After he has fallen asleep, she reaches over to rub his forehead, but when he turns his head slightly, she quickly pulls her hand away. Matt's dancing body, kissing mouth and licking tongue – even his head turning in sleep – all seem too active for Sandra, who can only be with a man when *she* is in total control. In a flashback to a dance party with other boys and girls, Sandra is a wallflower, too timid to join in. Particularly terrifying is a spin-the-bottle game that randomly matches a boy with a girl to do some kissing. Sandra can't bear the idea that Cupid's arrow might strike her, that love could be so out of her control. In part, then, whether she's able to realise it or not, Sandra's love of death would seem to be rooted in a fear of life: 'Necrophiles are frightened of getting hurt by normal sexual relationships.'[115]

Although Sandra may appear 'incapable of falling in love with a man who wasn't dead',[116] there is reason to believe that a live relationship is what she really wants. Why does she insist that the dead can still feel if she isn't looking for life in the corpses she has sex with? Why does she keep seeing Matt if there isn't something in a living boyfriend she desires? In one scene, Sandra lies atop fallen leaves in a cemetery while looking up at Matt, who is backgrounded by green trees above him. She brushes aside some dead leaves to reveal a gravestone and then he embraces her. It sometimes seems as though the necrophiliac Sandra is herself dead but hoping that Matt's love will revive her. Director Lynne Stopkewich has said that she thought of calling her film *The Kiss* but chose *Kissed* in order to convey 'not the kiss of life but not the kiss of death either'.[117] Sandra is in a liminal state, hovering between life and death, between Matt and the morgue. To meet her in the middle, Matt hangs himself so that she can make love to his dying body – and so that the last vestiges of his life can revive her dead desire: 'His star was the brightest I've ever seen, exploding and surrounding us.' By sacrificing himself and actively willing his total passivity, Matt shows Sandra that she does not have to be afraid of love, that he will kill himself before harming her, that she can safely entrust her body to his. But Matt is dead and so, ironically, his corpse – and those of subsequent young men – will now serve as a reminder of the love she lost and cannot find again. Just when she was ready to be kissed, the one soul she trusted is gone.

Ken Park (2002)

Directors: Larry Clark, Edward Lachman
Cast: Stephen Jasso (Claude), Mike Apaletegui (Curtis), James Ransone (Tate), Wade Williams (Claude's Father), Tiffany Limos (Peaches), Julio Oscar Mechoso (Peaches' Father), Harrison Young (Tate's Grandfather)

Claude, Curtis and Tate are three suburban California teens. Claude's father gets after him for being a skateboarder who wears jeans that sag below his boxers: 'Pull your pants up and wear 'em right. I look at you like that and I feel sick... because I'm ashamed. Your mother thinks you're a fairy.' But the father is actually ashamed of himself and his own homosexual desires, as seen when he crawls drunkenly into his sleeping son's bed one night and tries to give him head through the fly in the boy's boxers. The unwanted advances are so oppressive that Claude starts coughing, as if the assault prevented him from breathing.

In another scene, Curtis is about to receive fellatio from his girlfriend Peaches. Her father opens the bedroom door just at the moment when Curtis's erection pops up from his boxers as she is pulling them down. She hastily covers him up for protection, but her father throws her aside to punch Curtis in the face, bite his chest and strangle him until he loses consciousness. The father exerts a kind of castrating violence, as if to emasculate the boyfriend. 'Is Curtis a serpent?' the father asks her. 'Does he slither all over your unclean body?' By choking the life out of the 'serpent', Peaches' father would seem to preserve her purity, but the father has spoken of himself as having 'a serpent's tongue' and he then talks his daughter into becoming his own bride!

In the third plotline, Tate feels that his manhood is being stifled by his grandfather who, though outwardly loving, subtly belittles him by cheating to win at board games and by telling war stories of his heroic prowess. Tate takes his frustrations out on his barking dog, throttling the animal's neck with his hand and then tying a sock around its muzzle. However, the poor dog has only three legs, which suggests that, like Tate, it has been 'castrated', and so the boy is really just passing on the abuse to another damaged victim like himself. This he will do more directly when he chokes himself with a terrycloth belt that he has tied to a doorknob and wrapped around his neck while he sits masturbating – or 'choking the chicken' – with his back against the door. Tate's auto-erotic self-asphyxiation combines sex and death, taking grim pleasure from punishing his grandfather but using himself as a surrogate victim. Beating himself off, Tate both proves his manhood and comes close to strangling it to death. Later at night, Tate will crawl naked onto his grandfather's bed and stab him in the neck with a knife, getting an erection as he does so. It would seem that Tate has finally proven his greater prowess by sticking it to his grandfather. But it is important to note that when his three-legged dog starts barking, Tate goes soft again. A part of him realises that he is no less a victim for having become a victimiser – in fact, probably more so. Despite the phallic knife, he is still damaged and now lost in despair. Wearing his grandfather's false teeth which give him a frozen smile, Tate lies naked in bed with his pale and blood-spattered body looking like a corpse in the blue light. The scene is similar to the one where Tate's nude body lay there right after he ejaculated from choking himself. Tate has become his dead grandfather. The ecstasy of killing has led to the triumph of his own death.

Antichrist (2009)

Director: Lars von Trier
Cast: Willem Dafoe (He), Charlotte Gainsbourg (She)

A husband and wife make love while, in the next room, their three-year-old son climbs from his crib and then out an open window where he suffers a fatal fall. The scene is in black and white, as though it were already a flashback memory in which sex has been ruined by death. Extreme slow motion conveys the sense of time's inexorable passing along with a countervailing desire to slow it to a stop, to prevent the inevitable fall. There is an initial feeling of domestic normalcy and conjugal bliss as he and she grab some precious time while their child is sleeping to make love in the shower, the laundry room and the bedroom. Having sex with her husband standing and her seated on a counter next to the tumble dryer, she is both herself and a mother, taking care of her child's clothes while also satisfying her own desires – desires which in the past led to the conception of that very child. Droplets of water falling during their shower lovemaking, intercut with snowflakes falling as their child climbs onto the windowsill, create a sense of natural beauty and holy wonderment as both she and her child open themselves to the world in different ways, achieving different kinds of ecstasy. As her husband penetrates her against the shower wall or on the laundry-room counter, sex seems to lift her up, even as her child's teddy bear rises while lifted by a balloon. At the same time, her copulating body knocks over a toothbrush glass, displaces some puzzle pieces and causes a water bottle to spill, much as her son knocks a baby monitor with his teddy bear and sweeps some toy soldiers to the floor so that he can climb onto the table in front of the window. Seeking ecstasy and transcendence, her body and her son's exist in time and are susceptible, like other matter in this world, to gravity. Eden gives way to the Fall. After the death of her child, sex will forever be burdened with guilt for her. The scene makes it look as though her climax coincides with the moment her son's body hits the ground.

In a much later scene, while using her husband's hand to masturbate herself, she has another black-and-white flashback to the two of them making love, but this time her eyes are open and she sees her son climbing towards and falling out the window. Back in the present, she continues to masturbate desperately, weeping, and then uses some scissors to cut off her clitoris. In the extremity of her guilt, what she feels she should have seen and prevented has become a false memory of what she did see and is entirely responsible for not having stopped. Moreover, her innocent and natural pleasure as a woman has been contaminated by her mother's remorse so that she can no longer take pleasure in sex without punishing herself for it with pain. 'It was my fault,' she tells her husband. 'I could have stopped him. ...I want to die, too.' She and her husband are lying in their cabin in the woods – in an area known as Eden. Earlier, as they listened to acorns falling on the roof – 'falling and falling, and dying and dying', she had told him about how 'oak trees... only have to produce one single tree every hundred years in order to propagate'. Nature seemed utterly indifferent to all the acorns that fell and died: 'I understood that everything that used to be beautiful about Eden was perhaps hideous. Now I could hear what I couldn't hear before: the cry of all the things that are to die. ...Nature is Satan's church. ...Women do not control their own bodies; nature does.' Her son was the acorn that fell from her as Mother Nature, and she feels she must have been evil to pursue her own pleasure in a way so indifferent to his individual death. The force of sexual desire that moves through her seems more death-dealing than life-giving, more satanically selfish than maternally altruistic. Able to hear a child's wailing only as a death cry, able to experience sexual ecstasy only as excruciating pain, she has been exiled from Eden into a world that feels like a living hell.

TRANS

Liquid Sky (1982)

Director: Slava Tsukerman
Cast: Anne Carlisle (Margaret/Jimmy), Stanley Knapp (Paul)

New York City in the early 1980s. Margaret is a fashion model in the new-wave punk scene. Adopting an androgynous look, she doesn't believe in 'sexual definitions': 'Homosexual, heterosexual, bisexual – whether or not I like someone doesn't depend on what kind of genitals they have, as long as I find them attractive.' One man, Paul, views her assertion of sexual independence – 'I can come with or without you' – as a form of narcissism. If she's not particularly interested in *him*, it must be because she's in love with herself. 'Still sitting in front of the mirror?' he asks accusingly, when actually she is just applying make-up to her face (she *is* a model). 'I'm gonna show you the difference between men and women,' Paul says. 'I know you're wishing for a big, hard man.' When she tells him that she doesn't 'need [his] cock for anything,' he feels emasculated and decides that she must be a lesbian. In an effort to convert her to heterosexuality while also reaffirming his own manhood, he forces himself upon her: 'I'm gonna fuck you till you know what it means, dyke! ...You know you love it!' But Margaret is merely apathetic towards Paul's aggression: 'I'll lie down and you fuck me, see, because it doesn't matter to me, because you don't exist – you're nothing.' Rather than proving himself a big man through sexual assault, Paul is belittled, ignored, annihilated. In fact, Paul dies as he comes, obliterated by Margaret's obliviousness to him. (Ostensibly, aliens kill him, but the metaphorical meaning is that he dies when he can't pin down Margaret's sexuality, when he can't make her desire match his.)

In another scene, Margaret participates in a fashion shoot with a male model named Jimmy. In one pose, the two androgynous models stand back-to-back as if they were recto/verso sides of the same coin. The two look so alike they could almost be a single face and its reflection, as emphasised when both of them are doubled in mirrors as they are getting made up for the next photo session. (Their similarity was also evident in an earlier transvestism scene when Jimmy donned Margaret's dress and the two stood facing each other, a 'feminine' man and a 'masculine' woman. In fact, Margaret and Jimmy are both played by the same actress.) But rather than revelling in their likeness, insecure Jimmy is jealous of what he perceives as Margaret's greater beauty and fame. Calling her 'ugly' so that he can feel more 'beautiful', calling her a 'cunt' so that he can glory in his own 'cock', Jimmy asserts a hierarchical sexual difference between himself and her. Looking in the mirror becomes a way to see himself through society's eyes and to meet society's expectation that he be 'the man' and that she, as 'the woman', service him through fellatio: 'Jimmy liked what he saw. I don't look like her, he decided. ...She is shit and I am beautiful, he thought, and his cock swelled full. And she sucked it well, as a whore should, as he looked at his own great, handsome face.'[118] For Jimmy, the defining moment comes as he orgasms: he most fully masculine and dominant, she weakly submissive as 'the woman'. Rather than engaging in sex as a transgression of boundaries – a recognition of their equal beauty and self-worth – Jimmy falls from the ideal of androgyny and back into gender performance as 'the man' enforcing his sexual difference from 'woman': 'For a split second sympathy passed between them as he realised that she was like him. ...But the faces [of the photo crew] looking at him haunted him. They were waiting. Waiting for him to perform with her.'[119] And so Jimmy does – and dies like a man, literally perishing as he comes.

Transamerica (2005)

Director: Duncan Tucker
Cast: Felicity Huffman (Bree), Kevin Zegers (Toby)

Bree is a pre-op male-to-female transsexual who has just found out that she has a 17-year-old son, Toby, who doesn't know that she is his biological father. On a cross-country road trip, the two grow close. One night Toby enters Bree's bedroom. She pulls her nightgown up to more fully cover her breasts, saying 'I must look awful.' 'You look good,' he says, reassuring her about her newly developed female body, then adds, 'You look well,' trying to speak properly in front of her because she has been teaching him good grammar, like a mother. 'Don't worry,' she says, reassuring him about his grammar and his future; then, as he sits near her on the bed, she brushes aside a strand of his hair in a tender (maternal?) gesture. At this point, he leans forward and kisses her passionately on the mouth. She briefly responds in kind before pushing his face away, asking him – and also herself – 'Ah, what are you doin'?' 'What I'm good at,' he says, taking off his robe. Having survived on the streets by prostituting himself, Toby is confident about his physical appeal and his lovemaking ability. But when Bree protests, Toby hastens to add, 'It's okay – I want to. You'll like it – I promise.' Toby wants her to know that he is not hustling, that sex with her will be something he desires and that she will enjoy. 'I'll marry you if you want,' he says, indicating the depth of his commitment.

Toby then makes his most significant statement: 'I think you're sexy, Bree. It's like – like I really see you.' This is what Bree has always wanted: to be seen for who she really is inside and not just superficially or prejudicially. For Bree, this means being seen as the woman within and not as the man whose external form she still partly has. Toby knows that Bree has a penis and female breasts, and Toby desires him/her, recognising his/her transgendered body as parts of a continuing story about Bree's soul. In the words of the Dolly Parton song which closes the film, 'Well, I can't tell you where I'm goin'/I'm not sure of where I've been/But I know I must keep travellin'/Till my road comes to an end.' Some years ago, Toby's mother killed herself (he found her body) and his stepfather sexually abused him. As he tells his stepfather during a bitter reunion, 'I know what you missed. You missed my mouth. You missed my ass. You wanna fuck me right here?' Bree, who also once almost committed suicide in despair, has become the loving mother Toby lost – the mother he feels he can save and who can save him. At the same time, Bree is the father Toby never had, someone who can separate sexuality from violence and re-attach it to love. It is Toby himself who willingly kisses Bree on the mouth and who, acting on his own desire, stands naked before Bree, offering his body to him/her. And Bree behaves in the way Toby's stepfather should have: knowing that she is Toby's father, Bree does not have sex with him; she does not commit incest. Instead, she tells Toby the truth about his paternity and insists that the two of them must pursue a loving, non-physical relationship. Thus ends a scene which director Duncan Tucker has described as being 'so delicately balanced between sweetness, sadness, shame, embarrassment, sexiness and humour'.[120]

XXY (2007)

Director: Lucía Puenzo
Cast: Inés Efron (Alex), Martín Piroyansky (Alvaro)

In a Uruguayan fishing village, Alex is a 15-year-old intersex person, born with both male and female genitalia. A surgeon has come to explore the possibility of operating on Alex so that her anatomy will be unambiguously female. Alex gradually grows close to the surgeon's teenage son, Alvaro. While Alex, though raised as a girl, exhibits a certain 'masculine' forwardness and aggression, Alvaro is tentative, artistic and rather delicate-featured. His father fears that Alvaro may be 'a fag'. As their similar names suggest, Alex and Alvaro form a likeness across their differences, with both the masculine 'girl' and the feminine boy being gender – and possibly also sexual – nonconformists. When the two virgins make love in a barn loft, it is she who pulls him down, embracing and kissing him with her lying on top. He then takes the initiative in getting them undressed, motioning for her to remove her sweater, peeling off his own shirt and reaching inside her tank top to feel her breasts. 'I don't have anything,' she says, somewhat defiantly but also worried that she is not womanly enough to meet his expectations; but he reassures her with 'I like it'. It is not clear – nor does it have to be – whether Alvaro's desire is for a small-breasted female or a boy's body: that is, whether he is hetero- or homosexual or something in-between. Alex slides down Alvaro's jeans, pulls her own shorts down and then rolls him over onto his stomach, penetrating him and engaging in anal intercourse. Later, fearing that her active sexuality may have been overly aggressive, unwanted by Alvaro or the cause of pain, Alex apologises to him: 'Sorry about what I did to you.' But he, though a man, says he 'liked it', having enjoyed being the receptive partner, even as he had earlier enjoyed extending his hand into her tank top.

While some members of society may view this kind of sexual activity as 'unnatural', Alvaro has seen one turtle climb onto the back of another much as Alex mounted him, and it is known that the sex of some sea turtles is not genetically fixed but fluid under the influence of the environment. Similarly, the clownfish in the aquarium in Alex's room are sequential hermaphrodites, capable of changing sex over time. If nature is the example of what's 'natural', then Alex – and Alvaro's relationship with her – should be accepted as such. It is interesting to note that, as the two engage in sex, Alex wears a necklace with a turtle tag. She had given Alvaro a similar tag, telling him that 'these two are from the same family', but he refuses to wear his until the end, when he is finally ready to admit that loving her makes him as different – subject to social opprobrium and ostracism – as she is. It is at this point that Alex, for the first time, dares to open her pants and show him her male and female genitals. Alvaro, by recognising his affinity to difference, by wanting Alex just the way she is, has proven himself worthy of this sight. As director Lucía Puenzo has said, 'The film... includes the possibility that anybody (a virgin like Alvaro in this case) could fall in love and be aroused by a body like Alex's. Perlongher, one of my favourite poets, used to say: "We do not want respect; we want to be desired."'[121]

YOUTH

Love Strange Love (Amor estranho amor) (1982)

Director: Walter Hugo Khouri
Cast: Walter Forster (Adult Hugo), Marcelo Ribeiro (Child Hugo), Xuxa Meneghel (Tamara), Vera Fischer (Anna), Tarcísio Meira (Osmar)

Brazil 1982 and 1937. As an old man, Hugo remembers the two days he spent as a 12-year-old boy in a luxurious mansion where his mother worked as a high-class whore. One of the younger prostitutes, Tamara, pretends to be 'a virgin', looking 'innocent' and 'scared of everything'. In this, she is like Hugo who stares wide-eyed at the women's nudity but closes the door when they approach him. Tamara calls attention to her and Hugo's similarity ('Your eyes are prettier than mine') and to his liminal state between youth and adulthood: 'You'll be a big boy soon, but you're already quite something.' By dressing up in a white teddy-bear costume for a striptease number and then offering herself to Hugo, Tamara makes sex continuous with child's play, acting like a transitional object from maternal to sensual love. 'I'm a present for someone,' she tells him. 'Do you want to play with me? See how soft I am,' she says, placing his hand on her breast and having him squeeze it, 'so soft, so soft'. Later, Tamara will come to him in bed, taking off her teddy-bear costume and opening his pyjama top to lie with her breasts pressed up against his chest. In this way, she unwraps both their bodies as presents which she wants them to give to each other, like two children discovering their sexuality together, the difference between male and female breasts.

As for Hugo's relationship with his mother Anna, the two of them used to be very close, sharing a bond reminiscent of the time before his birth when they were both one. Indeed, they still bear a remarkable likeness to one another, as an onlooker notes that 'he's prettier than his mother'. Hugo has been separated from Anna for a whole year and now he finds out that his mother is a prostitute. Metaphorically, the film seems to be dramatising a boy's coming to sexual awareness ('One year – incredible – you're almost a grown man') and his new understanding of his mother as a sexual being. After taking a bath ordered by Anna, Hugo now covers his genitals with his hands as he steps out of the tub and his mother wraps him in a towel. Later, he watches her brush her hair in front of a mirror – something that he must have seen her do a hundred times as a boy – but this time he looks down and sees a growing erection. His question – 'Can I sleep with you?' – is beginning to take on a different meaning, as is his wish to have his mother all to himself and not to see her go with any other man. Spying through a grate while Anna is in bed with a client named Osmar, Hugo sees this naked man on top of his mother, hungrily kissing her neck and repeatedly slapping her across the face during the throes of passion. Does the son misinterpret sex as violence, owing to his ignorance of intercourse, his concern for his mother or his jealousy of this man? Or does Hugo actually see his mother being brutalised and does he worry that this is what sex is? That night, Hugo masturbates in bed while imagining himself making violent love to a prostitute, pinning her arms to the side while he thrashes about on top of her, even as he remembers Osmar topping Anna. However, Hugo also imagines himself lying on his back while a group of prostitutes overwhelms him with their kisses, as Anna looks on. Here the son has put himself in his mother's place, feeling what it is like to be the recipient of such aggressive advances – the opposite of before, when he had imagined himself as the sexual aggressor. In this way, Hugo tries to distance himself from sadistic sex and to preserve the loving bond he has with his mother.

As soon as Anna can arrange it, she plans to send Hugo away, realising that being around the degraded and degrading sex in a brothel 'wouldn't be good' for him. But Hugo cannot bear to be parted from his mother; he cannot stand for her to stay there and be subjected to further degradation. It is at this point that Anna makes a difficult decision: she makes love to her son. Opening her nightgown, she lays his head upon her bare breasts, then bends down to kiss him on the lips. With his naked body entwined around hers, he kisses from her breasts down to her sex, and she leans forward to wrap him in her arms, enfolding him. With this act, Anna is both mother and lover to him, wanting to show that there can be continuity between maternal and sensual love. His return to the womb is also a new discovery of the female sex, an initiation into adult sexuality, as she 'births' him into manhood. Anna wants to show him that she is not at heart a prostitute and that sex does not have to be degrading. She wants him to know that she will always love him, even though they must part – as all mothers and sons must, to go on to be with others.

Lolita (1997)

Director: Adrian Lyne
Cast: Jeremy Irons (Humbert), Dominique Swain (Lolita)

Cannes 1921. 14-year-old Humbert discovers sexual love with a girl his own age, but she dies of typhus. New England 1947.

The adult Humbert, fixated on certain young girls who remind him of his first love, falls for 14-year-old Lolita. He marries her mother and, after this woman dies, he has Lolita all to himself. In one motel-room scene, Lolita is seated and reading the comics in a newspaper. This innocent image of girlish enjoyment is lit by sun shining through a nearby window. As the camera moves closer, we discern that she is sitting on Humbert's lap, with his body mostly in darkness, his head thrown back. As the screenplay puts it, 'For a moment, we cannot quite see what is going on… [Lolita] is totally engrossed [in the comics], but her hips are moving, and we gradually realise they are making love.'[122] The screenplay goes on to note: 'There seems no dividing line between her sexual pleasure and the pleasure she takes from the comics.'[123] It is true that Lolita's face moves smoothly from smiling and giggling at the funny papers, her girl's retainer visible in her mouth, to panting and moaning with her head leaned back and her eyes closed – the posture of a woman in ecstasy.

But Lolita is not a grown woman, and while children have a right to explore their own sexuality, this should be at their own pace and with their own age group, as was once the case for Humbert himself back when he was a boy. Now the adult Humbert has prematurely accelerated a young girl's erotic experience, using her to satisfy his own obsessive desire for the first love he lost. This solipsism is shown by the fact that a (shirtless) Humbert is wearing pyjama bottoms and a (bottomless) Lolita is wearing Humbert's pyjama top, as if she were a mere extension of his sexual fantasy. Children have will and agency, but it is not clear that Lolita knows she is having sex or even realises what sexuality is, so in what sense has she given consent? This lack of awareness is another implication of there being for her 'no dividing line' between reading the comics and engaging in intercourse. It is Humbert's responsibility to make her aware of this dividing line, not to keep her in the dark about it. In all his relations with Lolita, Humbert has persisted in blurring lines: a 'paternal' arm laid over the back of her side of a love-seat, an 'I missed you' used as the excuse for a passionate hug, and the news of her mother's death exploited as a reason to give her sexual 'comfort': 'We made up [that is, they had sex] very gently that night. You see, she had nowhere else to go.'

The fact that Lolita is stuck with Humbert is emphasised by the flies trapped and wriggling on the fly-paper in the motel room where her sweaty body writhes on his lap. The flies – with their connotation of dirt, disease and death – suggest the soiling of her virtue and the corruption of her innocence. (It is interesting that Lolita later refers to her time with Humbert as 'all that muck', as if retrospectively realising that she was mired in something degrading.) One fly lands on a woman's face in the newspaper comic Lolita is reading and she shakes it off, as if unconsciously trying to rid herself of corruption. This fly buzzes as Lolita turns the page to see a cartoon of a daughter standing next to her father, who is shaking the hand of another girl with a boy her own age beside her. Some part of Lolita must want to be that other girl, happy in a teenage romance, rather than the daughter being used and besmirched by her 'father'. The motel's grimy floral curtains, the peeling paint on the ceiling and Lolita's chipped, red-painted toenails all indicate that Humbert has drawn her into a degrading act. No matter what he thinks, they are not 'making love'.

Bad Education (La mala educación) (2004)

Director: Pedro Almodóvar
Cast: Daniel Giménez Cacho (Manolo), Ignacio Pérez (Ignacio), Raúl García Forneiro (Enrique)

Spain 1964. Boys from a religious school are on a country outing. While a paedophile priest (Father Manolo) has his favourite boy sing a Spanish version of 'Moon River', that boy (Ignacio) longs to join his schoolmates who are playing together in a nearby river. In lyrical slow motion, a boy dives into the water. Two boys swim side by side and their arms gradually synchronise. Together they jump up out of the water, plunge back down under it and then leap up again. Swimming becomes a figure for children's first immersion in physical pleasure, a time when boyhood friendship slides into sensual play. For Ignacio, however, this time is marred due to molestation by a religious authority figure, who threatens to instil in the boy a sense that sex is sinful. So Ignacio's sensual song about the river is also filled with fear ('I won't be swept away by the water') and his natural desire to take the plunge into sexual discovery is countered by a sense of condemnation for dark and dirty deeds: 'River and moon, tell me where to find my God and good and evil/Tell me, I'm longing to know what is hidden and you'll find it –' Ignacio stops singing at this point because he has been made to feel the priest's erection. We infer this because the boy cries out 'No!' and comes running out from behind a large bush, with Father Manolo right after him, buttoning up his cassock. In addition, the short story on which this film was based is explicit about the enforced masturbation, even noting that the priest's pubic hair felt 'like dry grass in a field'[124] – something which is perhaps symbolised by the bush 'covering' this traumatic event and which is certainly the opposite of the wonderfully wet and sensual river. Director Pedro Almodóvar, who was himself a boy singer abused by priests, has said that 'sex should be discovered naturally, and not brutally, suddenly. For two or three years, I could not be alone, out of pure fear.'[125]

Some time after this riverside incident, Ignacio walks to a cinema with his friend Enrique. On their way there, a baby in his mother's arms reaches out and touches Enrique's face, and the two boys, who have been flirting with each other, laugh. Their growing affection is blessed by innocence, not corrupt like the priest's desire. Inside the darkened theatre as the boys watch the beautiful Sara Montiel on screen, Enrique reaches over and touches Ignacio's erection, and the other boy then returns the favour, with the two of them engaged in mutual masturbation. As Almodóvar notes, unlike the sexual abuse between priests and boys at the school, 'What was happening between students was different, because you consent to it'; this was sex being 'discovered naturally'.[126] But religious repression and sexual abuse – both forms of 'bad education' – have made Ignacio fear that such touching is a sin, while on screen the Sara Montiel character, who was raped at a convent, wonders aloud 'if I did something I shouldn't have'. That night in the boys' dormitory, Ignacio is kept awake by a combination of guilt and desire, confessing to his friend that he liked what they did but that 'it was a sin and God's going to punish us'. Sure enough, an angry and faux-righteous Father Manolo discovers the two boys clinging to each other in a toilet stall, their erotic excitement confused with their terror of his punishment for their 'sin'. To save his beloved Enrique from the priest's jealous wrath, Ignacio offers himself to Father Manolo in a Christ-like gesture of self-sacrifice. Ironically, in an attempt to preserve his ideal love for his friend, Ignacio prostitutes himself – not that he really has a choice – and thus sinks further into a sense of sex as contaminated by sin.

Birth (2004)

Director: Jonathan Glazer
Cast: Nicole Kidman (Anna), Cameron Bright (Young Sean), Danny Huston (Joseph)

After grieving the death of her husband Sean for ten years, Anna is finally ready to marry again – until a ten-year-old boy shows up, claiming to be Sean and telling her she should not marry this other man. As Anna and Sean eat ice-cream sundaes in a diner, she asks him if he's 'ever made love to a girl', and he says that she would 'be the first'. It is as though Anna were on a first date with the boy, returning to a time of budding romance. As director Jonathan Glazer notes, 'We hit on the idea of the fairytale – it was... so full of hope and innocence.'[127] Then Anna and Sean ride together in a horse-drawn carriage through New York's Central Park, just like a young couple falling in love. Back at Anna's apartment, while she is naked in the bath, Sean removes his clothes as she watches every step of his stripping down. The boy takes off his pullover sweater and shirt, slips out of his shoes, undoes his belt and unzips his trousers, pulling them off. He then peels off his white socks and slides down his white underpants, stepping naked into the bath to join her. Anna stares steadily at him, finally asking, 'What are you doing?' 'I'm looking at my wife' is his reply. According to Glazer, 'The place where the audience really squirms, or leaves the cinema, is when the boy takes off his clothes to get into the bath with [Anna], and I just hold the shot. You can feel the walls shake. It was entirely unsexy but it was important if we were going to take this woman all the way we needed to.'[128]

Anna wants to believe that her dead husband has returned to be with her, that the boy is a wish-fulfilment fantasy of her man come again. As Glazer notes, the child actor playing Sean was cast because of 'something very adult in him – and something very vague, which allows Anna to imbue him with what she wants'.[129] Not only does the boy Sean allow Anna to relive those early days of happiness with the man who became her husband, but the boy also arrests time, enabling her to deny her husband's death along with another harsh fact about him: she seems to have sensed that, before he died, he was having an adulterous affair with another woman. The boy's striptease is *not* sexy: it answers Anna's need to remember her husband as a fresh-faced innocent forever faithful to her as his first love. Sex (the lust which caused him to stray) and death (which caused him to 'abandon' her) have no role in her fairytale fantasy where Sean is her Prince Charming, the one love she can trust. It is during sex with her fiancé, Joseph, that Anna tells him that the boy Sean 'said I shouldn't marry you'. The thought of marrying again, of sexually consummating her love, reminds Anna of her husband's betrayal. Why should her fiancé be any more worthy of trust than her husband was? It feels much safer to remain attached to a boy whom she can see as the perfect counterpart to her girlish idealism. Indeed, Anna and young Sean look amazingly alike with their close-cropped hair and delicately childish features. After all, there is a sense in which he is a figment of her imagination, projected in answer to her needs.

But there is another important way in which the boy's removal of his clothes is not sexy: though his disrobing is filmed like a striptease, this Sean cannot satisfy Anna's desires – because he is only a boy. In a later scene, young Sean sits naked in the bath, but this time his face and body are dirty. 'I'm not Sean,' he tells Anna, 'because I love you.' Pure love is a childish fantasy. Adult desire involves the body and its sometimes dirty lust and betrayals. In this scene, Anna is told that she has to grow up. If she wants to be fully satisfied, she will have to risk loving a man with a sexy and potentially treacherous body like her own – and leave the dream boy behind.

Me and You and Everyone We Know (2005)

Director: Miranda July
Cast: Natasha Slayton (Heather), Najarra Townsend (Rebecca), Miles Thompson (Peter), Brandon Ratcliff (Robby)

Heather and Rebecca, both age 15, are walking behind 14-year-old Peter when Heather says, 'If you don't stop following us, I'm gonna scream', which she does. The scream suggests a fear of sexuality, but the fact that *they* are following *him* shows their desire for it. They *want* to scream, but in excitement, not fright. Their accusation of him as a stalker is flirtatious, a way of approaching the thing they're also trying to avoid. Back at Peter's house, the girls have oral sexual contact with him, but they protect themselves by deploying a battery of physical and psychological defences. The fellatio is framed as a contest between them as to which one can do it better. In this way, sex with a boy is kept as something between girls, and even though it threatens to separate them (if one is superior and thus more adult), the contest ends most satisfactorily: Peter can't tell any difference between them, so even after 'sex' they can remain the same girlfriends as before. The girls approach their first sexual experience as a team, each giving the other courage to continue, and the two come out together, in the end, apparently no worse for wear, which is greatly relieving. Heather even warns Rebecca to 'Get away!' when Peter is about to 'scooge', thus saving her friend from an aspect of male sexuality which, as girls, they both still consider to be disgusting. During the blow job, they require Peter to keep his face covered and his hands to himself. There is a sense in which the two, while taking the first step into sexuality, nevertheless preserve their virginity, for, if the boy can neither see nor touch them, then he hasn't 'taken' them, has he? Besides, everyone knows that blow jobs don't count as 'real sex' – but they count enough for the girls to feel that they have proven themselves capable as future lovers. This is something *they* did and can feel proud of, not something that was done to them or that took anything away from them. The peppermint candies they suck afterwards are the perfect symbol of the girls' in-between state: expertly freshening their breath after fellatio, the two are also enjoying a candy treat together just as they have always done as children.

In another plotline, Peter and his younger brother Robby sit at a computer and engage in an instant-message sex-chat with some anonymous adult woman. When Peter explains that 'bosom' means 'titties', Robby's first thought is 'Where's Mom?' For a six-year-old, breasts still have a primarily maternal connection. Having already wondered whether the woman in the chat room 'likes baloney' (and he means the actual sausage, not slang for the male member), Robby turns from eating to excreting and shares a fantasy with the online woman: 'I'll poop in your butt hole and then you will poop it back into my butt and we will keep doing it back and forth with the same poop forever.' Peter is concerned that this fantasy sounds both childishly immature ('We have to sound like we're a *man*') and too grown-up ('She's gonna think we're a crazy, perverted person. ...We're probably gonna get arrested'). However, the fantasy is a success with its female recipient. She likes its wild departure from the usual porn clichés: 'You are crazy and you are making me very hot.' She likes its tender reciprocity and promised fidelity: 'back and forth... forever'. And she likes its daring defiance of adult sexual norms, which tend to disparage anal eroticism: 'I have a finger in my asshole and it feels so good. I feel like I could tell you anything and you wouldn't judge me.' All of this is what she *reads into* Robby's fantasy, but what he intended by it is anyone's guess. No longer an infant and yet far from a man, Robby would seem to be in a liminal state of incipient awareness – between toilet training and coprophiliac sexuality? Certainly, the sophistication that this woman ascribes to him is lacking. Robby's seemingly clever emoticon –))<>((– is merely a literal depiction of 'pooping back and forth', and when the woman asks the typed question of whether he is 'touching' himself, Robby replies 'yes' only because his thumbs are touching as he rests his hands on the keyboard desk! This is a rare film that treats childhood sexuality with a sense of humour rather than as a tragedy. As director Miranda July has said, 'The fact that children are sexual and exist in an adult world is so terrifying, and yet... it's not inherently evil. Things do not have to go wrong. There can even be points of connection.'[130]

Melissa P (2005)

Director: Luca Guadagnino
Cast: María Valverde (Melissa), Primo Reggiani (Daniele), Elio Germano (Arnaldo)

Fifteen-year-old Melissa's sexual self-discovery begins when she holds a mirror up to her body, caressing her bare breasts and reaching her hand down inside her panties to touch herself.

'I'm filled with a feeling of love and admiration for myself,' thinks Melissa in the novel on which this film is based, and she has similarly idealised imaginings of what her 'first time will be like' with a boy, hoping that she will 'cherish a memory that forever remains beautiful'.[131] When her dream date, Daniele, rescues her from a pool, offers to teach her how to swim and then leads her into an Edenic garden, all seems idyllic. 'You want to kiss me?' he asks, but just as their lips are about to meet, he pushes her to her knees, pulls down his swim trunks and brings her face to his crotch, saying, 'Then kiss my dick.' Melissa's loving spirit is confronted with stark physical reality, which includes the 'love handles' and the 'pimples' on the boy's 'butt'.[132] (A shot that was ultimately cut would have shown 'his semen dripping from her mouth' as further evidence of 'the violence that she was a victim of'.)[133] But Melissa still maintains her erotic fantasy of a Daniele who will answer her desires. While climbing a pole in gym class, she climaxes thinking of him: 'How strange, I feel my body much more than before. I like it, but with him I'd like it even more.' On the night that Melissa offers him her virginity, Daniele does kiss her on the lips, tenderly taking down her bra and moving carefully into position between her legs on the couch. However, this romantic encounter – presented in slow motion – suddenly gives way to brutal realism as he grabs her ass and begins violent thrusting. Melissa tries to maintain the dream by keeping her eyes closed and repeating 'I love you' to herself, but finally even she finds herself forced to say aloud, 'I don't love you.' He calls her an 'idiot' for thinking that any of this could be about love, and the two of them stare at her hymenal blood on his fingers – the physical sign of her painful defloworing and the disillusionment it has brought in its wake.

At their next rendezvous, Daniele has Melissa close her eyes while they are kissing so that he can surreptitiously substitute his friend Arnaldo's mouth and tongue in place of his. But Melissa goes him one better, having vowed to prove that she is not a 'baby' any more with romantic dreams, but more callous and cynical than the guys: 'I will treat them all the same, not caring for their feelings, not caring who I have in front of me.' Ripping off Arnaldo's belt, she masturbates him while leaning over to lick the nipple and face of Daniele, who is seated next to his friend on the couch. She then hikes up her skirt and straddles Arnaldo, riding him right in front of Daniele. Of course, Melissa's violence is a sign that she does still care which guy she is with: she hopes that Daniele cares enough for her to be jealous, his soul outraged to see her body with another man's. But at the same time Melissa is taking in the males' indifference, beginning to lose her loving spirit as she gives herself over to indiscriminate lust. In another scene, she allows Arnaldo to blindfold her while she kneels and fellates a series of anonymous men: 'Five of them. Sucked them all. Strong excitement. Bad grade. Like a real slut.' Now, when she looks at herself in the mirror, she 'no longer saw the image of that girl who took such delight in examining herself... I saw a mouth that had been violated so many times... I felt invaded, fouled by foreign bodies.'[134] And her own body has become foreign to her, a maw of lustful flesh devoid of personality or spirit.

It is interesting that when Melissa does finally find a boy capable of appreciating her, he seems highly idealised, someone who draws sketches of her and kisses her – on the cheek! 'I abandoned myself in his arms,' she thinks, 'and he held me more tightly, kissing me with a passion that wasn't sexual desire, but a yearning for something else, for love.'[135] Sex and the body still seem too threatening, so love must transcend the physical altogether. One can't help feeling sorry for that girl who once examined her developing body in the mirror: doesn't she have a right to sexual desire along with her romantic dreams?

EROTIC ACTS

ANAL

I Love You, I Don't (Je t'aime moi non plus) (1976)

Director: Serge Gainsbourg
Cast: Joe Dallesandro (Krassky), Jane Birkin (Johnny)

Gay garbage man Krassky goes to a truck-stop diner and falls for Johnny, whose ass Krassky admires from behind. The only problem is that Johnny is female, as she reveals when she turns around. 'Oh, shit,' Krassky says, for he has a phobic reaction to women, as seen when he points to a discarded toilet and jokes with his male partner, 'Can you imagine all the vaginas that sat on this?' When Krassky gets between Johnny's spread legs, he goes soft, unable to have vaginal intercourse, and she kicks him out of bed, calling him a 'faggot'. This epithet angers Krassky, either because he doesn't like to be insulted, or because he has internalised society's homophobia and doesn't want to be thought of as gay. However, when Johnny presents her ass to him, saying 'I'm a boy', Krassky is able to penetrate her anus, finding fulfilment in that way. But Johnny shrieks so loudly from the pain that the two are thrown out of their hotel room by angry tenants whom they have awakened. These evictions keep recurring, and Johnny complains that it is not her fault if Krassky's buggery causes her to cry out in suffering. Johnny puts on a dress, claiming her right as a woman to do so ('I'm a girl, you see, shit!'), and though Krassky initially disapproves, he eventually smiles and tries to accept her. Earlier, Krassky had said about a dump site that 'this pile of shit is beautiful' and it would seem that he is attempting to love Johnny despite her femaleness, which would normally repel him. At the same time, Johnny is trying to find pleasure in anal intercourse because of her love for Krassky. After he has accepted her in her dress, she lifts it over her female face and bends forward over a bed so that he can take her anally. This scene segues into one where Krassky embraces Johnny from behind in the back of a dump truck while sodomising her. For the first time, she achieves orgasm, feeling his loving arms around her, while he comes inside her boyish behind, knowing that she is a girl but loving her nonetheless.

Summer of Sam (1999)

Director: Spike Lee
Cast: Mira Sorvino (Dionna), John Leguizamo (Vinny), Lucia Grillo (Chiara)

New York City 1977. After dancing romantically at a nightclub with his wife Dionna, Vinny sneaks off to have anal sex with her cousin Chiara: 'He fucks her in the ass,' says John Leguizamo (who plays Vinny). 'He can't do all that nasty stuff with Dionna, because she's a good Catholic wife. So he does it with everyone else. As long as he ain't married to them, he can treat them like hos.'[136] Anal sex excites Vinny in numerous ways that heterosexual monogamy in the missionary position does not. Sodomy is a sin – *peccatum contra naturam*, the sin against nature. It is brutishly lustful, similar to the way animals do it. It seems anonymous and can be painfully violent, enabling the penetrator to feel manfully dominant over women as weak and degraded whores. But Vinny's view of buggery makes him feel as guilty as it does engorged. When he sees the corpses of a couple killed by the Son of Sam near the place where he buggered Chiara, Vinny believes it is a warning from God to stop his sodomy or be killed for his sin: 'Some sick side of me had to drive Dionna right past the spot where I was just stickin' it up her cousin's ass, you know? Shit! And that's where I saw the dead bodies.' Now anal intercourse becomes linked to the faecal and the fatal, scaring Vinny straight back into his conventional marriage.

At the same time, Vinny tries to bridge the gap between wife and whore by following a friend's advice: 'Why don't you just tell Dionna you like these things and maybe she'll do it?' After Dionna grinds her ass against his crotch on the dance floor, seemingly showing a willingness for back-door action, Vinny takes her to a sex club where, as he buggers another woman, his wife reaches climax while sandwiched between another couple. Unfortunately, conventional morality and jealousy get the better of Vinny, who condemns Dionna for enjoying the very act he would like to commit with her: 'Did he fuck you better than me? ...You're a fuckin' whore!' Dionna then gets at the root fear (and secret desire?) of Vinny, calling him a 'faggot-fuckin' hairdresser' and telling him that she'll get 'a soul brother with a big black dick' to 'kick your ass and then I'll fuck him': 'Stick it up your fuckin' ass!' The notion of himself as limp-dicked and ass-penetrated is Vinny's worst nightmare (and most hidden wish?), the opposite of himself as dominant bugger.

BESTIALITY

The Beast (La bête) (1975)

Director: Walerian Borowczyk
Cast: Lisbeth Hummel (Lucy), Elisabeth Kaza (Virginia), Pierre Benedetti (Mathurin), Sirpa Lane (Romilda)

Religious repression makes physical desire seem animalistic and so, in this film, sex is literally figured as bestial. American heiress

Lucy has her 'virtue' guarded by prim and proper Aunt Virginia, who fears that Lucy's fiancé, Mathurin, is one of those French who have 'always lived in lust'. Indeed, after watching horses copulate in Mathurin's stable, Lucy is inflamed enough by the stallion's erection and the mare's pulsating vagina to put her own hand between her legs from behind and masturbate. Lucy's true 'animal' nature is suggested by the fur coat she wears and by the dark pubic hair visible through her transparent white wedding gown. In a dream, Lucy imagines herself as an aristocratic lady (Romilda) who runs after a lamb that has strayed into the woods and that gets bloodily clawed and devoured by a bear-like beast. Will the taking of her virginity on her wedding night make Lucy a lamb going to the slaughter? But the dream continues when, after the beast's claw leaves a red slash on her thigh, Romilda hangs from a tree branch as the creature buries its devouring jaws between her legs. Fearful cries become ones of passion as Romilda finds that she enjoys being eaten out. Still, when the beast later grabs her from behind, Romilda faints in terror, unable to countenance such powerful desire which she can only experience as an unwanted assault. Yet when she awakens to find herself being taken from behind by the beast, she licks her lips and moans. An aroused Romilda now gives full expression to her 'animal' nature, throwing off her own corset, squeezing the beast's cock between her breasts and mounting him in a frenzy of unrestrained lust. The beast climaxes – and dies, literally. Beauty has killed the beast. Does the film remain afraid of female sexuality as something so strong that, once unleashed, it will destroy the male? Does religion return in the end to mete out death as the punishment for 'beastly' desires, whether male or female? After burying her beloved beast, Romilda covers her breasts with her arm and puts a hand over her sex, walking slowly out of the woods. Like Eve exiled from Eden, she now seems ashamed of her nakedness and her desire which, at least for a brief time with the beast, had once seemed so 'natural' to her.

Fur: An Imaginary Portrait of Diane Arbus (2006)

Director: Steven Shainberg
Cast: Nicole Kidman (Diane), Robert Downey Jr (Lionel)

New York City 1958. Wealthy socialite Diane, shown plucking a stray eyebrow hair in order to maintain her conventional beauty, is attracted to Lionel, a man covered from head to toe in thick hair due to hypertrichosis, aka 'werewolf syndrome'. With her hair pinned up and her blouse buttoned to the top, Diane has often longed to let her hair down and expose her bare breasts to a man wild enough to recognise her own animalistic desires. 'Have you ever met a woman who was just like you?' she asks Lionel, offering herself as his savage soul-mate even though she would appear to be his depilated opposite. As Diane takes photos of Lionel, 'there's a tremendous sexual element that you feel in her pictures, her relationship to the subject', explains director Steven Shainberg. 'And you feel her touching her subjects, in the way that you might touch a fur. So there's a way in which she's connected to sensuality and the beast. You could say that her whole life, her whole body of work, was beauty going out into the world to find beasts, and touch beasts.'[137] Ever since she was a little girl, Diane has identified with the small animals that her furrier father killed for their coats to adorn wealthy women and make them look beautiful. Now, by loving Lionel, Diane is finally able to touch and embrace those outcast animals that her parents had forbidden her to feel or feel for. Lionel 'is, in some sense, an animal... that animal that she thought about and might have cared about and might have been connected to'.[138] When Diane lathers and shaves off Lionel's body and facial hair, she thrills at the contact with his 'animal' nature while at the same time accepting him as fully human, stroking his newly revealed and finely featured face. After his death, she wears a coat he made for her from his own hair, for she is no longer afraid to expose the wild desires and empathetic sensuality that he brought out in her.

Zoo (2007)

Director: Robinson Devor
Cast: Russell Hodgkinson (H), John Paulsen (Mr Hands), Ron Carrier (Happy Horseman), Jenny Edwards (Jenny)

This film presents itself as a documentary about a secret community of men who have sex with horses. According to director Robinson Devor, 'There are very few subjects any more that are quote-unquote *dirty* to the average person, subjects that a filmmaker could endeavour against all odds to make beautiful. And this was one of them. I just felt there was some love in this story.' Devor says that he was trying for 'an aesthetic beauty wedded to this outrageous concept, this idea of merging with an animal'.[139] The zoophiles or 'zoos' believe that they 'love the horses'. The numerous *H*s in the Internet names used by the men – H, Mr Hands and Happy Horseman – show their self-perceived affinity to the horses. Of course, this linguistic likeness is not one that the animals themselves, being illiterate, can appreciate. For the Happy Horseman, 'The sex was just a small component. By standing there talking to them, in a way you're kind of connecting to them, going "I'm talking to you on the same level that you're kind of staring at me, mammal to mammal".' Except that, surely, rather than a mammalian bond across the man/animal divide, this horse's stare could as easily be one of incomprehension at this strange creature – man – speaking a foreign tongue. Mr Hands used to 'take off his clothes as a sign of solidarity with the horses he owned',[140] but if the animals have no sense of themselves as being naked, can they share this solidarity with a stripped-down human? The Happy Horseman believes that, during sex with a horse, 'You're connecting with another intelligent being who is very happy to participate, be involved,' while another man asserts that 'in their mind, they don't care whether it's a filly underneath them or a human. You've got something like a male animal – pretty much our purpose on this earth is to procreate.' Are the horses making a special connection with another intelligent being or just blindly procreating with any available body? The men don't know, but each projects his own erotic fantasy onto his equine 'partner'. 'Maybe I just want to grab a horse by his nuts and to feel his balls,' says H, clearly caught up in a fantasy of superior animal potency with which he would like to connect. Mr Hands keeps a cast of a horse's cock in his apartment. While the zoophiles claim an inside knowledge of horses, the men believe that anyone who criticises *their* behaviour is ignorant. About a horse rescuer named Jenny, H says 'she doesn't know her ass from a hole in the ground when it comes to horses'. However, it is one of the men, Mr Hands, who dies from a perforated colon after being anally penetrated by a horse. Was he so deeply engaged in a fantasy of inter-species bonding that he failed to see what he didn't know about the dangerous differences between man and beast?

CUNNILINGUS

The Cooler (2003)

Director: Wayne Kramer
Cast: Maria Bello (Natalie), Alec Baldwin (Shelly), William H Macy (Bernie)

Casino waitress Natalie is used to being disrespected by men. 'How'd you like to birdie that hole?' is what boss man Shelly asks Bernie, as if Natalie's sex were the prize object in a macho game. Shelly pays Natalie to be Bernie's 'cooze companion', reducing her to an oozy cunt or cum bucket. (And women who won't put out when men pay them to deliver are like the slot machine referred to as Marnie 'because she's one frigid broad' – like the cold blonde in the Hitchcock film.) Natalie is attracted to Bernie because he seems less boastful and domineering than other men, but initially his insecurities make him equally self-centred. After struggling to undo the snaps on her white leotard, he overcompensates by rolling on top of her in bed and thrusting wildly between her legs, which results only in premature ejaculation. As director Wayne Kramer notes, 'This [first] sex scene is about [Bernie] getting his rocks off.'[141] Afterwards, though, as the two lie side by side, Natalie cups Bernie's genitals in her hand, reassuring him that 'You've got a great cock.' Encouraged by her, he reaches over to hold her sex ('You've – Thank you'), almost but not quite brave enough to give her a matching compliment. Their second sex scene together begins with a close-up on Natalie's face in orgasm, which a subsequent shot of Bernie's head between her legs reveals was given to her by cunnilingus. Now he is confident enough to focus on *her* pleasure. It's not about him or his penile prowess, not about what he can prove to himself or other men. As actress Maria Bello (who plays Natalie) has said, 'A woman deriving pleasure from [cunnilingus] is very scary for a lot of people,' adding that 'men take their penises very seriously.'[142] Bernie is finally man enough to realise that he can bring her pleasure without using his.

In the Cut (2003)

Director: Jane Campion
Cast: Meg Ryan (Frannie), Mark Ruffalo (Malloy), Nick Damici (Ritchie), Jennifer Jason Leigh (Pauline)

English teacher Frannie is looking for the lavatory in a bar basement when suddenly she witnesses a scene of fellatio. The kneeling woman's mouth on the man's erect penis shocks Frannie with the directness of its intimacy. Later, Frannie masturbates to her memory of this oral pleasuring, but she does so while lying face-down on her bed and while still wearing panties, 'the cloth interceding between my fingers and my vagina, interceding between shame and pleasure. Perhaps I was afraid that I would die were there not a piece of cloth, something intervening, to prevent me from falling irrevocably into a trance of self-delighting.'[143] When Frannie then meets her dream guy – the man she thinks she saw being given head, he turns out to be a foul-mouthed police detective named Malloy, whose misogynistic banter makes her fear that he merely uses women as sex objects. When his buddy Ritchie says, 'That chick wants to suck your dick – all you need are two tits, a hole and a heartbeat,' Malloy replies, 'You don't even need the tits,' and Ritchie counters with, '*You* don't even need the heartbeat.' Frannie's sister Pauline has some less than encouraging words to say about men's egocentrism and insensitivity to women: 'I can remember every guy I ever fucked by how he liked to do it, not how I wanted to do it.' No wonder Frannie is reluctant to remove her panties when the time comes to make love with Malloy. However, seeing that he has disarmed himself, taking off his gun and lying back full-frontally exposed on the bed, she allows him to take down her underwear. She still lies face-down on the bed, but when he begins to eat her out from behind, she arches in passion, looking over her shoulder at him in surprise that he would do this for her and reaching her hand back to stroke his hair while he is licking: 'He sucked my clitoris into his mouth. There was nothing intervening. Not a nightgown. Not even a penis.'[144] He takes her other hand in his, companionate in touch as well as tongue. Her foot flexes in orgasm, just as it did when she had masturbated earlier while thinking of her dream guy, an erotic fantasy that seems to have come true.

The Wayward Cloud (Tian bian yi duo yun) (2005)

Director: Ming-Liang Tsai
Cast: Sumomo Yozakura (woman), Kang-Sheng Lee (man)

A woman in a white nurse's outfit lies on a white bed, while wedged between her spread thighs is a red half-watermelon. A man in a white doctor's coat puts his head between her legs and begins lapping at the fruit, with the woman writhing and moaning as if he were licking her sex. He then proceeds to finger the fruit, squishily poking faster and faster in and out of the hole at its centre as the woman's gasping increases until she cries out, mouth open in orgasm. The watermelon juice he squeezes between her breasts seems to figure his climax as well. Although the man and woman are actors making a porn video, this scene appears more positive than most. In place of 'split beaver' and 'cum' shots, there is the playful indirectness of a watermelon wedge and sprayed juice. 'Playing doctor' returns them to a childlike innocence, as does the joy of eating a succulent watermelon, with its bright red colour standing out against the white. 'Eating out' a woman is represented as something delectable and *her* enjoyment is emphasised along with his, with the pleasure not being merely phallocentric. Indeed, the woman licks her lips as though the man's tongue on her sex were an extension of her own, his lapping a part of her own self-satisfaction. In stark contrast to the playful cunnilingus here is the film's final scene, where the porn camera captures the man as he brutally fucks the woman, even though she is comatose or dead. Now the pleasure is hardly mutual. This phallic objectification of a woman's body continues when the man then forces fellatio on another female, causing her to gag when he comes.

FELLATIO

Intimacy (2001)

Director: Patrice Chéreau
Cast: Mark Rylance (Jay), Kerry Fox (Claire)

Every Wednesday afternoon, Jay and Claire meet at his dingy flat. They don't know each other's names. They barely speak. They just have sex and then she leaves. During one such encounter, Claire takes Jay's flaccid penis in her mouth, going up and down on it to make it hard, while he simultaneously has a hand under her dress, fingering her. She then masturbates him to orgasm, but when he puts his face between her legs, she pushes his head away, saying 'It's all right', and leaves. This scene made headlines for containing the first graphic depiction of fellatio between a non-porn actor and actress in a mainstream film. As director Patrice Chéreau explained, 'The point was not to stop at the moment where films usually stop and introduce an ellipsis. If we'd cut away, paradoxically it would have been just another sex scene. But now you see the difficult attempts of two bodies to unite when these characters don't know each other.'[145] Indeed, the very fact that the actor and actress are actually engaged in fellatio works to dramatise the distance between their characters, the sense that their physical intimacy is counterpointed by an emotional estrangement, a 'professional' gap separating them. The sex is real but it is also a 'performance', with the actors – since they are actors – never completely involved in the moment with one another. Yet they *are physically* connected, as the oral sex graphically shows, and the shock of seeing mainstream actors engaged in real sex becomes the shock of seeing any two people trying to use bodily intimacy to connect emotionally. Her awkward effort to get him hard and his rebuffed attempt to reciprocate the oral sex show the difficulty of moving from sexual to emotional intimacy. In a further paradox, the actors playing the scene have said that they could never have given this performance, which includes actual fellatio, if they hadn't talked to and genuinely cared about each other – the very things that their characters find it such a struggle to do: 'We talked about being good to each other, and kind, open and honest. That we must always tell each other exactly how we felt.'[146] Perhaps for this reason, the *desire* to communicate comes through, even when – or because – the sex seems to founder in the merely physical.

Battle in Heaven (Batalla en el cielo) (2005)

Director: Carlos Reygadas
Cast: Marcos Hernández (Marcos), Anapola Mushkadiz (Ana)

Middle-aged Marcos works as a driver for a rich man with a 20-something daughter, Ana. Marcos has known her since she was a child. Marcos confesses to her that he perpetrated a botched kidnapping in which a child died. Ana has sex with Marcos. After they disengage, she prolongs their physical contact by brushing the back of her hand against his, telling him, 'You'll have to turn yourself in.' Marcos appears ready to do so but then changes his mind and stabs Ana to death with a knife so that she cannot tell on him. He thus takes the life of another 'child'. Trying to be penitent, Marcos shuffles on his knees as part of a pilgrimage to the Virgin of Guadalupe but then collapses inside the basilica. It's not clear whether he is mortified by sin or saved through penance.

The film begins and ends with explicit scenes of Ana on her knees fellating Marcos. Director Carlos Reygadas has expressed his belief that 'many people will see beyond a simple blow job': Ana and Marcos are 'having sex and it's meant to be a close relationship, but it doesn't seem it. ...All this for me contains a whole world of frustration and longing for something better.'[147] The opening scene represents a fantasy of cross-class and inter-generational contact. Marcos may be poor, old and overweight, but a beautiful young woman from the upper classes deigns to kneel before him and show him loving attention. At the same time, there is a sense of distance between them: the back of her head, with its dreadlocked hair, is more visible than her face; a condom covers his penis as she takes it into her mouth; and tears fall from her eyes during the act. It's as though, in being responsible for the death of that child, he feels himself unworthy to see her face, to be fully accepted, to inspire joy rather than sadness. And yet this Virgin's faith in him, her willingness to love him despite his sins, her sorrowful recognition that the flesh is weak – these move him to remorse for his misdeeds and lead him to seek forgiveness. In the scene at the end of the film, Marcos is granted an unobstructed vision of Ana's whole face as she accepts his flesh into her mouth without a condom. As he smiles down at her, she looks up lovingly at him. In this heavenly moment of his imagination, all separateness has been overcome, including that between flesh and spirit.

Shortbus (2006)

Director: John Cameron Mitchell
Cast: Paul Dawson (James), PJ DeBoy (Jamie), Peter Stickles (Caleb)

Ex-street hustler James has been in a monogamous relationship with Jamie for five years but will not allow himself to be penetrated. For James, sex has been tainted by the abuse he received from former johns: love 'stops at my skin. I can't let it inside. [Jamie] loves me as hard as the people who treated me like shit.' In the opening scene, James lies on a yoga mat, pulls his legs up over his head and attempts to lick his own dick. Rather than being narcissistic, this auto-fellatio represents James's struggle to let himself be loved. In being both penetrator and penetratee, James can practise making love in an environment where he has total control and cannot be injured by another man. At the same time, though, James's self-suck remains partially motivated by fear: it excludes his lover and may continue to remind James of degrading past experiences such as when he was used as a dumping ground. After James comes in his own mouth, he lies there abjectly on the floor, his body convulsed with sobs. Rather than learning how to love himself, James seems to have been taken back to a time when being abused made him feel unworthy of love. He tries to kill himself, leaving film of his auto-fellatio as a suicide note. But a neighbour (Caleb) who witnessed James's attempt at self-love, recognising it as a cry for help, rescues him and the two of them have sex, with James on the receiving end. Caleb's penis thus becomes the transition between James's own and his lover Jamie's, moving James towards an acceptance of sex as conveying love. The auto-fellatio was the first step in this process.

MASTURBATION

Law of Desire (La ley del deseo) (1987)

Director: Pedro Almodóvar

The off-screen voice of a director orders a young actor to strip but to leave his underpants on. Although the voice commands compliance, reticence and resistance are part of the fantasy; the eye cannot yet see all. The actor is told to look at himself in a mirror and to kiss his own lips, pretending that they are the director's. Narcissus is led from self-love to a desire for the other. Lying in bed, the actor is to play with his nipples and caress his cock – and not just for his role in this movie: 'Do it for real. You've got to get turned on.' If auto-eroticism is a kind of pretence, an imitation of love, then the actor must move towards true passion, a real longing for another. Now the actor is told to remove that last barrier, his underpants, and to kneel on the bed: 'Reach between your legs and caress your ass. ...Now ask me to fuck you.' That bubble of self-love must be penetrated, moved from masturbation to intercourse, to real receptivity.

However, even as the actor mouths the words ('Fuck me. Yes. I'm going to come'), they are actually spoken by a dubber, a man standing next to the director and voicing lines from the script. The actor does appear to come but from jerking off, not from making love to any other. Finally, the actor is paid for his performance, which is like that of a prostitute who has masturbated for a voyeuristic client. And the director, by writing his own erotic script and then manipulating the actor to conform to it, is the most narcissistic of all. He is the one who has not moved beyond a masturbation fantasy.

Coming Soon (1999)

Director: Colette Burson
Cast: Bonnie Root (Stream), James Roday (Chad), Gaby Hoffmann (Jenny)

You would think that privileged preppie Stream would know about masturbation and orgasms, but ignorance and repression of female sexuality are still so widespread that even she, with her culture and education, lacks this intimate understanding of herself. Her boyfriend Chad tries to convince her that she comes when he does, and at first she believes it. But what she feels with him is not the orgasm she reads about in *The Hite Report*: 'a dam-breaking burst of piercing pleasure and muscle spasms, followed by trembling and diminishing shudders'. While not connecting with this bookish description with its overwrought clichés and tortured physiological specifics, Stream does realise that she is missing out on something big. She is, however, discouraged from finding out what this is. A phallocentric culture turns her interest away from discovering herself and towards pleasing a man. (Even in French class, she is taught to repeat, 'I adore the croissant, but I prefer the baguette.') Her friend Jenny thinks of women who masturbate as 'pathetic' and 'desperate' loners who must not have boyfriends. And Stream herself is so passive and repressed that she can barely work up enough interest to pleasure herself: 'Every time I try, I just get bored and fall asleep.' And yet one day, partly by accident and partly because she is increasingly open to new experiences, Stream finds that if she positions herself just so, a jacuzzi water-jet pulsing between her legs will bring her to orgasm. As she wriggles around in wide-eyed amazement at feeling such pleasure, a shot of the jacuzzi water spraying frothily signifies her climax. It could be said that Stream discovers herself in that jet stream, that auto-eroticism opens the way to female sexuality for her. As director Colette Burson says, 'I wanted to plant this idea in young girls' heads that you have a right to have an orgasm, you have a right to sexual pleasure.'[148]

Destricted (2006)

Director: Gaspar Noé

Gaspar Noé's segment of this short-film anthology cross-cuts between a man and a woman, each masturbating in a separate bedroom. The woman is in pigtails and clutches a fluffy teddy bear, whose head she kisses and holds to her breasts and between her legs while she touches herself. Her 'little girl' fantasy is romantic and softcore, involving tender companionship as the way to fulfilment. Among the other toy animals on her bed is a green frog: perhaps she is dreaming that one day her prince will come? The man, on the other hand, masturbates using a blow-up sex doll. After stuffing his cock in the doll's rear and mouth holes, he jerks off while pumping a gun in and out of her mouth, building towards the moment when he 'shoots'. His 'bad boy' fantasy is one of screwing her into submission, of violence as the means to 'a brutal climax'.[149] On his wall is a poster that says 'This is the Enemy', which is the way he treats the female sex. Despite the cutting back and forth between them, there appears to be no bridging of the gender gap between these two incompatible fantasies, one girlishly romantic and the other violently hardcore. If the man and the woman were actually having sex, would he fantasise about her as a sex doll while she is dreaming that he's a teddy bear? Does the difference in their fantasies mean that sex itself is masturbation? The title of this short film is 'We Fuck Alone'.

18-Year-Old Virgin (2009)

Director: Tamara Olson
Cast: Karmen Elena Morales (Chelsea), Todd Leigh (Spencer), Olivia Alaina May (Katie), Dustin Harnish (Ryan)

Morning in suburban America: three houses, three high-school teens, each of whom is masturbating while thinking of another. Sitting on her bed in a see-through nightgown in front of a mirror, Chelsea works her hand between her legs, saying 'You're so hot!' While the ostensible object of her fantasy is a boy named Spencer, the scene makes it clear that Chelsea is infatuated with herself. Here masturbation has its traditionally stigmatised sense: narcissism.

In another bedroom, Spencer's auto-erotic fantasy also contains egocentric elements, but at least it does truly feature another character besides himself: his beloved, Katie. As an avid video-gamer, Spencer incorporates aspects of his favourite pastime into his fantasy, having Katie vigorously work the joystick on a video console while bent over to display the cleft between her legs. 'You get into that groove,' she says, simultaneously playing a great game and encouraging him to enter her. 'It's all in the grip,' she adds, allowing him to imagine that she holds his joystick when in fact he is the only one with a hand on himself under the bedcovers. In his fantasy, Katie straddles his cock, telling him that 'I've been thinking about you all day on top of me, fucking me so hard you make me scream.' It is interesting that she is the dominant one while telling *him* to get on top; she is aggressively sexual while wanting *him* to get hard. Somewhat touchingly, the virginal Spencer needs her active encouragement in order to be able to perform, which shows that he isn't just one big, inflated ego.

For her part, virginal Katie's masturbatory dream involves a Harlequin-romance scene with a guy named Ryan, a Fabio lookalike with bared chest, a red rose, and the wind in his hair. Katie's fantasy goes straight from making out with him to their spooning together in bed, eliding the sex entirely. As a comical comment on the dream's unreality, a vibrating toy mouse finds its way under the bedcovers and into Katie's crotch, furthering her childish fantasy that intercourse will be just a pleasant tingle.

MENAGE A TROIS

The Ages of Lulú (Las edades de Lulú) (1990)

Director: Bigas Luna
Cast: Francesca Neri (Lulú), Oscar Ladoire (Pablo), Fernando Guillén Cuervo (Marcelo), María Barranco (Ely), Rodrigo Valverde (Pablito)

Lulú falls in love with Pablo, the best friend of her brother Marcelo. Pablo buys her a vibrating dildo, which she inserts in her panties like a cock. Excited, he bends her over and takes her anally, hurting her. Later, in a three-way with a transvestite (Ely), Pablo has Lulú go down on him while watching Ely spread his own legs and play with his penis. In another scene, Pablo blindfolds Lulú so that, unseen by her, Marcelo can enter the room. Using scissors, the two men cut holes in the front and the rear of her panties, then take her in a double penetration: 'Their penises moved in unison inside me. I could clearly feel them both, their tips meeting, brushing against each other through what felt to me like a flimsy membrane, a thin wall of skin which was in danger at every thrust... they're going to tear me and then they really will meet, one against the other.'[150] In this threesome, Pablo uses Lulú to consummate his desire for Marcelo, with no concern for what it costs her physically or emotionally. At the moment of climax, he removes Lulú's blindfold and she sees to her horror that she has in fact committed incest with her brother.

In some ways, Pablo himself has acted like an abusive father towards her – 'a bad daddy, perverted, incestuous'. He initiates her into sex at a young age, giving instructions and dictating her every move. When she grows older, he shaves her pubic hair so that he can maintain the thrill of corrupting a minor: 'I like little girls with little girls' cunts, especially when I'm about to debauch them.'[151] But, as Lulú ages, she grows increasingly desperate to hold his interest, even making love to him in front of Ely so that Lulú can imagine herself as the sole object of Pablo's attentions, excluding all others.

However, following the scene in which Pablo and Marcelo jointly abuse her, Lulú begins to engage in other threesomes for quite different reasons. In one of these encounters, a dominant man brutally takes an effeminate boy from behind in order to force the boy's cock into Lulú's vagina. It is no accident that the boy's name is Pablito. In this scene, Lulú can imagine herself screwing Pablo in the way that he has screwed her: 'I wanted to possess him. It was an unprecedented feeling. ...To be on the other side of the road, on the pavement with the strong. ...Now he was just an animal, a beaten, mistreated dog, infinitely desirable.'[152] At the same time, Lulú also feels sympathy for him, recognising the boy's subjection as similar to that which she has suffered under Pablo: 'I had seen dozens of women in that same posture. Including myself... I would have liked to talk to him and tell him: *Older men sometimes have strange ways of loving. I know how you feel*.'[153] For Lulú, this threesome becomes a way that she can find compassion for herself and seek the strength to dominate Pablo, the overbearing man in her life.

Bully (2001)

Director: Larry Clark
Cast: Nick Stahl (Bobby), Brad Renfro (Marty), Bijou Phillips (Ali), Rachel Miner (Lisa)

Bobby pushes his friend Marty to perform in an amateur striptease at a gay nightclub. Naked except for his boxers, Marty is at first awkward and embarrassed, but as he grows less self-conscious, he eventually enjoys gyrating and thrusting his hips. Bobby is left watching with the men in the audience who can neither be nor have Marty. The friends go on a double-date with two women, Ali and Lisa. While essentially forcing Ali to give him head in the front seat, Bobby looks behind to see Lisa willingly spread her legs so that she and Marty can enjoy intercourse in the back seat. Whereas the surfer Marty is at ease with his own body and comfortable enough with his sexuality that he draws both men and women to him, the nerdish Bobby repels everyone with his insecurities, hating his own homosexual side and overcompensating as a macho heterosexual. Watching Marty with Lisa, Bobby can imagine that *he* is the thrusting hetero stud and that *he* is the lover being penetrated, when in fact he is only a nerd who bullied another woman into giving him a blow job – an act which could be hetero- or homosexual and thus conveys Bobby's unhappy confusion over his sexual identity.

In another scene, after spitting at his own naked image in the mirror, Bobby enters his bedroom and sees Lisa riding Marty in bed. Bobby whips her with a weightlifter's belt so that she falls off and he is now positioned between Marty's legs. Punching Marty in the face, Bobby says 'I'm next' and, as Marty turns around to avoid the blows, Bobby is behind his bent-over body. What happens next is elided, but it's possible that Bobby rapes Marty or Lisa – or both. Feeling excluded from the comfortable sexuality that Marty and Lisa have, Bobby forcibly inserts himself, invading and destroying them. The love he cannot express comes across as macho violence.

Later, Bobby rapes Ali while forcing her to watch a gay porn video with him. 'You know that turns you on,' he says, while thrusting between her legs in the same position as the porn actor who is penetrating another man. 'Say I'm the best you ever had!' he orders her, slapping her until she repeats it over and over again. It is Bobby who can't admit that gay sex turns him on, Bobby who struggles to love a woman by imagining that he is with a man, and Bobby who, despite the repeated violence, can never believe he is man enough in bed.

Y Tu Mamá También (2001)

Director: Alfonso Cuarón
Cast: Diego Luna (Tenoch), Gael García Bernal (Julio), Maribel Verdú (Luisa)

Best friends Tenoch and Julio meet a voluptuous older woman, Luisa, and invite her to join them on a road trip. Before leaving, the two teens jerk off together on side-by-side diving boards, both coming at the same time when they fantasise about Luisa. Rough-housing in the shower, Tenoch tells Julio, who is uncircumcised, that he has an 'ugly dick' which 'looks like a deflated balloon'. 'So blow it up,' Julio counters, 'blow the balloon!' 'Back off, faggot' is Tenoch's reply. When Tenoch makes another derogatory comment about Julio's penis while in the car on the road trip, Luisa defends him, saying, 'I like hoods.' In this way, she mediates between the boys, leading them to overcome their dislike of their differences, which is really a mask for their fear of sameness, of homoerotic attraction. The boys reveal that they have measured each other's erections to see whose is biggest, only to find that there is very little difference between them. Beyond their rivalry, which defensively insists on difference, there is a desire to be accepted and loved. Eventually, each boy sleeps with Luisa in turn, provoking a jealous fight between them and prompting the question, 'Which of us fucks better?' But Luisa sees right through their macho competition, revealing the amorous desire it tries so violently to hide: 'Typical men, fighting like dogs and marking their territory! What you really want is to fuck each other.' Each boy claims to have screwed the other's girlfriend, but, with Luisa's mediation, even this violation of their manhood – 'You fucked my trust! You fucked my girl! You fucked me!' – becomes an occasion for homoerotic bonding: 'Yuck, I've been stirring your vanilla.' 'Me, too.' 'So we're milk brothers.' The boys go from sleeping with each other's girlfriends to sleeping with Luisa and finally to sleeping with each other. In a three-way scene, Tenoch puts his hand between Luisa's legs and then Julio eats her out. After kissing both boys in turn, Luisa takes down their pants and masturbates them while Tenoch and Julio passionately kiss one another. This kissing occurs on an idyllic beach called Heaven's Mouth which, like the love between them, neither boy even thought existed – until they met Luisa.

The Dreamers (2003)

Director: Bernardo Bertolucci
Cast: Michael Pitt (Matthew), Louis Garrel (Theo), Eva Green (Isabelle)

1968. Matthew is a conservative American staying with an unconventional pair of brother-and-sister twins, Theo and Isabelle, in their Parisian apartment. Matthew's love affair with the androgynous twins becomes an exploration of his own ambiguous sexuality. Young enough not yet to have been channelled into a clear-cut sexual identity, Matthew finds himself simultaneously attracted to both of them, with their threesome representing the revolutionary potential of a transgressive mode of sexual relations outside the social norm. In an early scene, while Matthew is peeing in the sink, Theo's pink toothbrush falls in – the same toothbrush that he will later put in his mouth to brush his teeth. The scene indicates Matthew's unconscious desire for Theo, along with Theo's 'girlish' willingness to be penetrated. Isabelle touches Matthew's 'ripe and red and luscious' lips, wanting to put red lipstick on them so that he will look like 'a pretty girl'. Later, after Matthew has taken her virginity, Isabelle's hymenal blood is transferred from his fingers to her face and then to his lips, as though *she* had deflowered *him*. (Indeed, he was a virgin before they made love.) Prior to this lovemaking, Theo grabbed Matthew from behind while Isabelle kneeled before him, pulling down his boxers to reveal his growing erection, under which he had hidden a photo of her in a red bikini. This exposure of his manly desire causes the timid Matthew to faint like a girl in Theo's arms. Upon awakening, Matthew at first thinks Theo is Isabelle: Matthew's desire is as much to be taken by the brother as it is to penetrate the sister. Later, sitting naked together in the bathtub, Matthew lets Theo lean over him to blow marijuana smoke into his mouth. At the same time, Matthew wants to penetrate Theo. After riding behind him on a motorbike, Matthew watches while Isabelle uses a feather duster to lift up Theo's shirttail and reveal his bare buttocks while he is masturbating to a photo of Marlene Dietrich. Matthew, who is wearing a woman's silk kimono, wants to be the female object of Theo's desire while also manfully taking Theo from behind. The sexual fluidity of the threesome is epitomised by the scene in which Matthew takes a banana from Theo and peels it like a foreskin on a penis, then sticks his finger into the banana's tip to create a hole, inverting the 'penis' into a 'vagina' or 'anus'. Michael's finger action also splits the banana three ways, giving each of them a piece to eat – in much the same way that they have all three shared each other.

NUDITY

Boogie Nights (1997)

Director: Paul Thomas Anderson
Cast: Mark Wahlberg (Dirk)

1970s Los Angeles. Porn star Dirk Diggler is, we are constantly told, tremendously well-endowed. 'A stellar sexual standout' is what the industry calls him, giving Dirk the adult movie award for Best Cock. We see co-stars and crew members looking stunned at the sight of it. When Dirk unzips, women grow wide-eyed and men stare in envy. We see the bulging crotch of Dirk's jeans. We see a poster on his wall of a giant snake wrapped around a man's leg. We see his magnificent orange Corvette with its extensive front hood. But we don't actually see 'the thing' itself until the end of the film, when Dirk stands in front of a mirror and pulls out his 13-inch dick. He *is* well-hung, but this dangling appendage fails to live up to all the hype, perhaps because no flesh is ever adequate to the fantasy we build around it. The big reveal proves anticlimactic as he just stands there with his flaccid penis hanging out, exposed as vulnerable flesh. 'I'm a star. I'm a star. I'm a bright, big, shining star,' Dirk repeats to himself in the mirror, trying to pump up his ego for the upcoming porn shoot, to project an image of phallic strength while fearing that the flesh is weak. The director, Paul Thomas Anderson, has said that he wanted 'the saddest happy ending I could come up with'[154], and this sizeable disappointment is certainly it. Earlier, while barely able to maintain an erection because he was high on cocaine, Dirk had defensively bragged, 'I'm the biggest star here, man. ...It's *my* big dick!' Then, fired from the shoot and replaced by another up-and-coming stud, Dirk tried prostituting himself but couldn't produce a hard-on and got himself gay-bashed as a 'little faggot'. By investing his entire sense of self-worth in his cock ('Everyone's blessed with one special thing'), Dirk pays the price when that prize possession is revealed to be subject to the same weaknesses as any other penis.

Cashback (2006)

Director: Sean Ellis
Cast: Sean Biggerstaff (Ben)

As a boy, Ben is startled by his first sight of a 'beaver shot' in *Hustler* magazine: 'The smiles on the girls' faces and the total lack of shyness about what they were showing the camera was confusing for me. I had never seen the female part up-close and in so much detail. I guess I imagined something neater, like a smooth hole drilled into a piece of wood, the sort of hole where you might place a wooden peg, but the reality was much more sexually aggressive.' Ben expected the woman to be compliantly receptive to his phallic confidence (a hole for his peg), not smiling impudently in the knowledge that she is getting paid to display herself, like the supercilious neighbour girl who demands money to drop her knickers before the eyes of slavering boys. When he is a young man, Ben's girlfriend breaks up with him, her eyes looking down on him while her mouth denounces him. In his job at a supermarket, Ben fantasises being able to stop time and, while the female shoppers are frozen, take down their bras and panties to expose their breasts and pubes. In so doing, Ben takes vicarious revenge on his girlfriend, making women vulnerable to his gaze as he was to hers. He can strip and spy on all these women while they are 'captured' and 'unaware', enjoying them voyeuristically when they cannot see him or challenge his sexual mastery.

But Ben is also a would-be artist who sketches these nude women, finding 'inspiration' in 'the female form' and looking for beauty in every aspect of their being. As a boy, he was enraptured with a girl who broke a limb and who, when the plaster cast was opened, revealed that she had a hairy arm. Like the 'beaver' on the unclothed magazine model, this hairy arm is not what Ben imagined he would see when that part of his girl was uncovered, but 'it only heightened [his] fascination [with] her'. If Ben's fantasised stripping of the female shoppers is an assertion of male mastery over them, his sketching of their bodies is also an attempt to come to terms with female sexuality, with the fact that the actuality of women exceeds his impoverished imagination and that women have their own desires which aren't a simple fit with the fulfilment of his. Ben is learning to see beauty in women *as they are*, not just as he has imagined them to be in his sexual fantasies.

Forgetting Sarah Marshall (2008)

Director: Nicholas Stoller
Cast: Jason Segel (Peter), Kristen Bell (Sarah), Mila Kunis (Rachel)

Men's concern about endowment and potency is serious enough that it tends to make full-frontal male nudity a rare occurrence on screen. 'America fears the penis,' says producer Judd Apatow, 'and that's something I'm going to help them get over. ...I'm gonna put a penis in every movie I do.'[155] This is one such film, featuring a character aptly named Peter. After a shower, Peter lowers the towel that was wrapped around his waist to shake his thing in front of his girlfriend, Sarah – a self-consciously silly moment of macho bravado. However, when he finds out that she is breaking up with him, he drops the towel altogether, letting his flaccid dick dangle and putting his hands over his eyes. He doesn't want to see her leave nor does he wish for her to view him in this 'unmanly', humiliated state, and indeed she lowers her eyes as if the sight of his abjection were unbearably ridiculous. As actor Jason Segel (Peter) comments, women 'see a naked, out-of-shape man crying and it's funny – something weird, disturbing and disgusting we can all laugh at.'[156] When Peter then turns and bends over, weeping, his exposed asshole only completes his embarrassment. But Peter does turn around again and approach Sarah, leveraging this moment of weakness for sympathy and pleading with her to stay: 'If I put clothes on, it's over,' he realises, for then he will no longer be able to play the vulnerability card. (His display may also be a way of saying, 'Look at what you'll be missing' – and Peter is quite well-endowed, a 'show-er' not a 'grow-er'.) The two of them sit together on the couch while he pleads his case, but when Peter intuits that she's been seeing another man, he stands up confrontationally, his cock in her face, demanding to know who his virile rival is. After she rises too, he holds her in a standing hug, at once clinging pathetically to her and making a sexual claim to her body, as if to prove that he is man enough for her. She leaves him anyway.

This scene is reprised at the end of the film but with an ego-boosting difference. Peter's new love interest, Rachel, catches him in the nude and laughs while he hastily covers his genitals with his hand. However, she then walks up to him and engages him in a passionate embrace, with his naked body pressed up against her, followed by a song on the soundtrack that says, 'You took me by surprise and let me inside of you...There's got to be some part of me inside of you.' It would appear that Rachel finds his penis fulfilling, so he need no longer fear that it's a laughing-stock.

ORGY OR MULTIPLE PARTNERS

Score (1972)

Director: Radley Metzger
Cast: Gerald Grant (Jack), Claire Wilbur (Elvira), Calvin Culver [Casey Donovan] (Eddie), Lynn Lowry (Betsy)

Most porn films intended for a wide audience will show a man with a woman, a man with two women, and a woman with another woman – but not a man with another man. *Score* is one of the rare films to break this taboo, much to the surprise and dismay of certain viewers: 'This movie did NOT go where I expected it to!' 'Be warned: you heteros are barking up the wrong tree.' 'I was shocked. If you are a homophobic male or think such images might upset you, STAY AWAY!'[157] One reviewer cautioned that 'unprepared audiences may greet it with disgust or extreme discomfort.'[158] In fact, for years the only video of *Score* available was one in which the gay parts had been cut out, and this is still the version of choice for some: 'Avoid all the male-on-male sex and buy the censored version.'[159]

In their swanky villa on the French Riviera, liberated couple Jack and Elvira introduce newlyweds Eddie and Betsy to the swinging lifestyle. Drinks and drugs are deployed to loosen inhibitions, along with costumes and role-play to open up the other sides of the timid neophytes. Nerdy biologist Eddie dresses up as a studly cowboy, and convent-raised Betsy dons spike heels and black lingerie. Betsy catches her reflected image in a wavy mirror doing 'perverted' things *she* wouldn't normally do, such as touching Elvira's breast and letting Elvira go down on her. Similarly, Eddie finds himself looking at nude photos in gay as well as straight magazines, and an image of a man's hand down another man's pants is projected over Eddie's crotch when Jack screens an 8mm gay porn movie. As we cut back and forth between Jack seducing Eddie in the downstairs den and Elvira seducing Betsy in the upstairs bedroom, it becomes harder and harder to determine who is with whom – and who is male and who is female. As Elvira says about 'who's who' in the wild spouse-swapping she has engaged in, 'First you don't know, then you can't tell, then you don't care.' The wavy mirrors and wide-angle close-ups make the entangled bodies seem virtually interchangeable. At one point, we cut from Elvira in a strap-on dildo screwing a bent-over Betsy to Jack fucking Eddie from behind and then to *Betsy* screwing Eddie, the wife pegging her own husband. As a boy, Eddie used to 'mess around' with Betsy's brother – something he has missed since getting married but now can reconnect with via Jack's cock and Betsy's strap-on. Betsy, too, misses the physical closeness she once had with her mother and the secret sexiness she felt around the nuns, and these experiences can now be recaptured with the lovingly maternal Elvira, who also dresses up in a nun's habit – with skin-revealing slits down the sides. Thus the orgiastic exchange of partners becomes a way for this hetero husband and wife to overcome the melancholy loss of their earlier homosexual attachments.

But not everything about this sexual roundelay is so rosy. Thirty-something Jack and Elvira seem driven to seduce younger couples by the fact that they themselves are unhappy in their marriage, having grown tired of each other and increasingly desperate for new flesh. And, rather than being bisexual, Eddie may be a closeted gay. At the end, he seems to stay married to Betsy only for appearances' sake, while planning to have drunken and drugged-out sex with any man she invites into their bed – as long as the next morning Eddie can then 'forget' it ever happened.

Prick Up Your Ears (1987)

Director: Stephen Frears
Cast: Gary Oldman (Joe), Alfred Molina (Kenneth)

After receiving an award, playwright Joe Orton does not return directly to his domestic partner Kenneth to celebrate with the man who helped him achieve his success. Instead, Joe goes below ground to a gents' lavatory that is dark and dank: 'urinals... the more insalubrious the circumstances, the more Joe seemed to enjoy it'. He proceeds to have sex serially and simultaneously with multiple men, in extreme defiance of the heterosexual monogamous norm: 'The little pissoir under the bridge had become the scene of a frenzied homosexual saturnalia. No more than two feet away the citizens... moved about their ordinary business.'[160] Stepping up to a urinal, Joe unzips then turns to show his cock to the man standing next to him. Though Kenneth is loyal to him, Joe finds that being around his bald, older lover makes him fear his own loss of youth and sexual potency. Having his manhood admired by all these men in the gents makes Joe feel infinitely desirable and omnipotent. The men converge on him as the centre of attention, one going down on him and two at his chest, stroking and sucking his nipples. Others watch through peepholes in toilet-stall doors, witness to everyone's worship of Joe as a sex god. There is also the thrill and peril of danger. An undercover cop could arrest him and subject him to public disgrace, including the loss of his fame as a playwright.

Anonymous sex with multiple partners risks venereal disease, which could destroy his desirable body. And Joe is exposing himself to strangers, including rough trade that – instead of making him feel invincibly potent – could injure or kill him. According to biographer John Lahr, 'promiscuity was a submersion in chaos' for Joe, 'a flirtation with death, a ritual wasting with its "magical" corollary of renewed fertility. ...His trips into forbidden territory were the only alternative he saw to the quiet, cosy suffocation of conventional British living.'[161] While he may *love* Kenneth, Joe's *desire* is for other men. Perhaps the greatest emotional danger Joe runs is in splitting off sex from love, making him a totally un-integrated being – someone who is orgiastically torn apart.

Sex: The Annabel Chong Story (1999)

Director: Gough Lewis

This is a documentary about porn star Annabel Chong, who was filmed having sex 251 times with 70 men in ten hours for the X-rated movie *The World's Biggest Gang Bang*. Though some viewers may watch the movie with the aim of seeing Chong get royally screwed, her goal in making it was paradoxically self-empowerment. Having been gang-raped in the past, Chong uses the gang bang to relive the trauma but with herself in control this time, gaining mastery over the men. She has them checked for STDs, insists that they wear condoms and has anyone removed from her body if he displeases her. Chong also turns the tables on her aggressors, mocking the 'limp' men's 'nervous' attempts 'to get hard' from her queenly position of power on a bed atop a plinth.[162] (Chong's sexual performance is modelled on that of Roman empress Messalina, who is reputed to have made multiple men her conquests.) Chong even speculates about the 'homoeroticism' of the guys 'standing in line waiting, stroking their dicks, looking at each other's dicks'[163] – hardly the kind of thing that these men, there to prove their hetero credentials, would want to hear. In fact, Chong thinks of the '251'-count sexual marathon as an 'over-the-top parody of what men are supposed to be like – you know the idea of a stud who just wants to (sleep) with anything that moves. ...It was aimed at denouncing the male quantitative approach to sex'.[164] At the same time, in playing the 'stud' herself, Chong wants to 'really shake people up from all the stereotypes about women as being passive sex objects' and to assert 'every woman's right to express, flaunt or otherwise exploit her sexuality!'

But, with all due respect for Chong's sense of her own agency, one has to wonder about who is being exploited here. Chong's performance became the highest-grossing porn video of all time, but the male producer never paid her for it. Sex with all those men was sometimes 'claustrophobic' and the cause of physical 'pain'.[165] Not all the men wore condoms and, of those who didn't, not all had been tested for AIDS, prompting Chong to say afterwards that she felt 'terribly disturbed' and '*extremely* betrayed by the fact that they didn't take the health precautions I thought they did'.[166] In the end, the line between gang bang and gang rape seems to have blurred, making one more likely to fear for Chong than to celebrate her triumph.

Shortbus (2006)

Director: John Cameron Mitchell
Cast: Paul Dawson (James), PJ DeBoy (Jamie), Jay Brannan (Ceth), Peter Stickles (Caleb), Sook-Yin Lee (Sofia)

Unlike most cinematic orgies where the sex is loveless, frenzied and grotesquely sinful (*Satyricon*, *Caligula*, *Eyes Wide Shut*), this film's group sex aspires to be utopian. Rather than faceless promiscuity, there is a personal and polymorphous perversity, with all the characters in the cast making intimate connections in the 'magical circuit board' of desire that is the orgy room. James, the former hustler, is penetrated by his lover Jamie and can feel the sex as affection rather than abuse. Ceth can kiss James, the man he has longed for, while having sex with Caleb, the new man of his desires. As her husband watches her with loving eyes, Sofia can finally reach climax while sandwiched between a successfully orgasmic couple. To make the actor-participants or 'sextras' in the orgy scene feel more comfortable, gay director John Cameron Mitchell himself stripped naked and occasionally joined in the action, even engaging in cunnilingus for the first time 'as a gesture of solidarity'.[167] Yet, as Mitchell has said, 'In the sex room everyone is desperate, but it's funny. The audience laughs and cries all at once.'[168] Drag impresario Justin Bond comments that 'it's just like the '60s – only with less hope.' After 9/11, there is the fear of religious fundamentalism that would condemn the sexually liberated to death. There is AIDS which threatens to place a mortal limit on how freely individuals can 'connect' with one another. When Bond sings 'As your last breath begins/contently take it in/'cause we all get it in the end', the conflation of sex and death makes this an ambivalent orgy. With condoms freely available, must anal intercourse still be dreaded as a potential death sentence? With fundamentalism on the wane, can't the gasp of orgasm be enjoyed without fear of being condemned to an apocalyptic end?

PERVERSION

A Dirty Shame (2004)

Director: John Waters
Cast: Selma Blair (daughter Caprice), Tracey Ullman (housewife Sylvia), Johnny Knoxville (sexual leader Ray Ray)

A conventional town in middle America. When some citizens are hit on the head, they turn into sexual deviants. For example, after a concussive fall to the ground, a woman carrying a bag of groceries becomes a 'splosher' with a fetish for pouring food down her front and rubbing it all over her breasts. The film captures the way in which the particular things that turn us on often appear to be random and accidental – inexplicable attachments formed when we are suddenly receptive to them and the whole world seems eroticised. A sheltered daughter becomes an exhibitionist where she gets to show off her mammoth mammaries. A cop trades his uniform and truncheon for baby clothes and a pacifier, allowing him to express his less authoritarian side. A repressed housewife does a hoochie-coochie dance and 'pick[s] up a bottle with her cooter' in order to show that she, too, has desires. Perversions are fun! – especially when the deviant behaviour is 'safe, consensual and doesn't harm others', as the town's sexual leader advises.

But are perversions really so friendly and life-affirming? At first it may seem as though director John Waters has avoided confronting the dark side of deviancy. Here there is no bestiality with chickens, mother-son fellatio or eating of dog shit as there was in Waters' 1972 underground film *Pink Flamingos*. Given the eager-to-please perversions in *A Dirty Shame*, it might seem a little strange that Waters says he made the film to ask the question, 'Can tolerance go too far?'[169] A closer look, though, finds some revealingly troublesome moments in this otherwise wacky sex comedy. 'Funching' ('fucking after lunch') is one thing, but what about 'frottage', defined by one character as 'the sexual rubbing-up on unsuspecting citizens' – how harmless would you consider this to be if it happened to you? One nymphomaniacal woman tries to seduce a husband right in front of his wife and young son. Another woman, who is into erotic asphyxiation, joyfully strangles herself with a phone cord in a public booth. Without the structure provided by society's sexual norms and conventions, the townspeople become crazed sex addicts compelled to gratify their perverse urges no matter what the cost to their neighbours or themselves.

Even before these happenings, one character in the film says that 'tolerance' has already gone 'too far', and another notes that, for 'kids' these days, 'second base isn't just feeling up a bra strap any more. No, it's a blow job.' Waters has argued that the perversions in the film, which tend to be *alternatives* to oral-genital contact and intercourse, are 'safe' in that 'you can't get pregnant' and 'you can't get AIDS': 'If I was a parent, I'd hope [kids] were sploshing instead of giving blow jobs. I think you ought to hope your children are doing perverted sex acts with food.'[170] But there is a certain sadness and desperation in the characters' frenzied, driven search for alternative modes of pleasure in the age of AIDS. Waters says that 'when AIDS came along, people, gay and straight, had to figure out new ways to have sex', since 'sex had to be reinvented'. This is what led him to explore the notion of perversions and 'the idea of trying to think up a new sex act. Everybody wishes they could. We *need* some new ones.'[171] Curiously, when the characters finally do 'discover a brand-new sex act – one that's never been performed before', it consists of butting their heads together, thus deliberately bringing on the concussions which, before, had accidentally turned them on to a variety of perverse pleasures. The new sex act ends up being the desperate desire for new sex acts!

RAPE

Legend of the Overfiend *(Chojin densetsu Urotsukidoji)* (1989)

Director: Hideki Takayama

This film is the most notorious entry in the 'erotic grotesque' genre of anime porn. Nerdy college student Nagumo spies on Akemi changing in the women's locker room. His masturbation is nearly revealed when his orgasmic groans call attention to his presence.

Then, while watching Akemi perform as a cheerleader, Nagumo is helpless to stop himself from coming again, and this time his ardour is exposed to the mocking laughter of his classmates. Later, trying to overcome his shyness, Nagumo lets Akemi fellate him but ejaculates prematurely in her face. Nagumo's adolescent anxiety over being exposed as a wimp – not man enough to keep a woman happy – seems confirmed when suddenly a rival for Akemi's affections, Nikki, bursts into the room and steals her away. Licking some of Nagumo's semen off Akemi's face as if taking on his potency, Nikki grows a giant tentacle which snakes out from his crotch, making him monstrously macho. However, just as Nikki is about to rape Akemi, Nagumo himself sprouts multiple red tentacles which bind his rival and wrap around Nikki's neck, strangling him. Nagumo has defeated the competition with his superior phallic force, but now he fears that his penis is *too* powerful and will hurt Akemi if he tries to make love to her. Yet, after hiding naked in a closet, he is coaxed by Akemi to come out. He considerately asks her permission to penetrate her, which she lovingly grants, and the two seem united in bliss – until his eyes begin to glow red; his chest becomes heavily muscled; and his cock starts fucking her like a demon. In this world of teenage terror at the physical transformations brought on by desire, there seems to be no middle ground between shyness and lust, between impotence and rape.

Baise-moi (2001)

Directors: Virginie Despentes, Coralie Trinh Thi
Cast: Raffaëla Anderson (Manu), Lisa Marshall (Karla), Karen Lancaume (Nadine)

Manu and her friend Karla are gang-raped in a deserted warehouse. Included among the shots of men slapping and punching them are close-ups of vaginal penetration. It could be that these 'cock in cunt' shots, typical of hardcore porn, are here repurposed to repel rather than excite the viewer, especially since sounds of Karla screaming in pain are heard over them. However, for any viewer already inclined to get off on violent porn, the juxtaposition of pain and penetration is just likely to prove more stimulating. After the rape, Manu takes her revenge by teaming up with Nadine, another woman who has suffered abuse at the hands of men. Together they sexually torture their oppressors. With one man, Manu does a seductive lap dance, bringing his head to her breasts, but then bites his cock during fellatio, while Nadine watches, stroking her own breasts. The violence these women commit is sexualised and they seem turned on by it. Earlier, Nadine is seen masturbating to violent porn on TV, and Manu has been a porn actress. Now it is as though Manu is playing out such a scene in front of Nadine for her arousal. The perversely erotic scene reaches a climax when the two women kick the man's face in, leaving his head bloody red like an engorged phallus. Yes, the females are fighting back against abusive males, but has sex been tainted by violence for the women, too, because of the brutal treatment they received? After having seemingly 'normal' and pleasurable sex with a man in an alley, Manu feels strangely unsatisfied: 'Looking at the alley, she thinks about what she'd rather do here, fucking or carnage. While the guy was at it, she'd thought about [the violence she committed earlier]... As good as fucking. Unless it's that she likes to fuck as if it's a massacre.'[172] Nadine does an erotic dance in her black bra and panties, excitedly pointing a gun. Later, Manu sexually humiliates a man by making him crawl on all fours, grunting like a pig, then gleefully rams a gun up his rectum and shoots. How different is she now from the men who raped her? After Manu is killed in a shoot-out with another man, Nadine takes a gun and 'masturbates the barrel, caresses the metal as if she's making it harder and tighter, so it will go off in her mouth like lead come'.[173] The eroticisation of violence is ultimately self-destructive.

SADO-MASOCHISM

The Attendant (1993)

Director: Isaac Julien
Cast: Thomas Baptiste (the attendant), John Wilson (the visitor)

In this short film, a black museum attendant stands guard over paintings depicting white masters taking the lash to captured African slaves. The attendant imagines enacting a similar tableau in which he lies prone on the museum floor, his pants down and his black buttocks exposed, while a white male visitor stands over him with a whip. In another image, a white master in leather gear raises a whip and stands with a dildo behind a black slave's ass. Is it still reprehensible racist domination when it's transposed to the realm of erotic fantasy and dreamed by the black man himself? Earlier, in searching the visitor's bag at the museum entrance, the attendant had imagined finding a leather whip which he held near his own crotch as the visitor stroked it. Does the black attendant desire to be dominated by the white visitor's whip? In this sado-masochistic scenario, who has the phallus, or is it shared between them? Is this scene about violent dominance or tender desire, with the white visitor stroking the black attendant's cock? Note that the attendant also envisions another tableau in which a white man caresses the face of a slave in chains, as if in sympathy with his suffering.

As the fantasy continues, the question of dominance becomes further complicated by desire. The white visitor is accompanied by an angel with a pitchfork, as though ready to sadistically stick it to the black attendant. However, the attendant himself has an angel with a bow and arrow, poised to penetrate the visitor's heart. If the white man can be struck by desire in the same way as his black counterpart, are they not equally masochistic in the sense of being prone to love? One tableau vivant shows black angels aiming an arrow at the gold-lamé crotch of a white man, whose queer costume suggests that he might be receptive to it. In another scene, it is the white visitor who is now face-down on the floor with his ass exposed to the black attendant's lash. And behind the attendant is a painting in which a collared white guy on a leash enjoys being sodomised by a black man – and this from the imagination of a white artist, Tom of Finland. Could these erotic fantasies, where black and white exchange positions of dominance and submission, help bring an end to racial and sexual hierarchies in real life?

Killing Me Softly (2002)

Director: Kaige Chen
Cast: Heather Graham (Alice), Joseph Fiennes (Adam), Natascha McElhone (Deborah)

In this erotic thriller, Alice leaves her comfortably conventional boyfriend and has high-risk sex with Adam, a mysterious mountain-climber who time and again dangles her over the abyss (metaphorically speaking), but promises that he will never drop her. In one scene, he ties a white silk scarf around her neck and chokes her with it while thrusting upwards into her as she rides him on a polar bear rug. 'I gave up all control,' she says about the erotic asphyxiation. 'I let him decide when I could breathe and when I couldn't. I loved it.' But the air starts to get too thin for Alice as she begins to receive anonymous notes ('How far will you let him go?') and to suspect that Adam may have had a similar sado-masochistic relationship with another woman, Adele, whom he might have strangled when she tried to leave him. (The name *Adele* seems a strange contraction of *Adam* and *Alice*, which suggests that Adele is a figure for Alice's worst fears of what Adam might do to her.) When Adam binds her hands and feet to a wooden kitchen table, Alice thinks it is to stop her from leaving, but he accuses *her* of jealousy and masochism: 'Is the suspicion [of me with another woman] exciting? Do you need it to get off? …Did you sneak around behind my back because you need it to get rougher and rougher? If you do this, will I punish you?' As Alice lies there bound and gasping in her white nightgown, Adam puts his hand around her throat, saying, 'I could break your neck, I love you so much.'

Adam's sister Deborah admits that she sent the notes warning Alice to 'leave him for your own good'. But it turns out that Deborah, who had had a sado-masochistic relationship with her brother when they were young, is the one killing off Adam's girlfriends and now, jealous and possessive, she tries to murder Alice, too. When Deborah attempts to choke her to death, Alice fights back, eventually shooting her. In this way, Alice fights to overcome her own voluptuous desire to die at the hands of another, while simultaneously struggling to conquer the jealousy and possessiveness she felt towards Adam. In defeating Deborah, Alice tries to free herself from her own sado-masochism.

Secretary (2002)

Director: Steven Shainberg
Cast: Maggie Gyllenhaal (Lee), Stephen McHattie (her father), James Spader (Edward)

Lee's father has expected her to be the perfect daughter while molesting her since puberty. Internalising his abuse, Lee self-harms, using the sharp point of a ballerina figurine to cut into her thigh. Lee goes to work for an older man, Edward, as his secretary. Like her father, Edward demands perfection of her, using his thick red pen to correct 'genderr' when she mistypes the word in a memo and thus fails in her 'female' role, which is to be entirely submissive to his commands. Ordering her into his office, he has her bend over his desk where he gives her a wicked spanking as punishment for her error, and she takes pleasure in letting him. He shackles her arms to a spreader-bar and she seems to enjoy the crucifixion. He straps a saddle on her back and puts a carrot in her mouth, and his domineering mastery excites her.

Lee uses sado-masochism to contain and control the abuse she suffered from her father. He held her down and rode her against her will for years; it was an endless violation. But, with Edward, the bondage and domination do not exceed playful boundaries permitted by her; it is only what *she* wants. When Lee puts an earthworm in an envelope for Edward to find, she both strikes back at her father (having cut off his 'cock') and tells Edward that she wants his 'dirty dick', desires to be 'befouled' by him. What used to feel horribly degrading at the hands of her father is now something that she can enjoy taking from Edward: 'Cock. Place your prick in my mouth. Screw me.' According to screenwriter Erin Cressida Wilson, 'The secret to real submission is that the submissive is really the one in charge. ...What if she were to stop fighting it and instead she embraced it, defined it and then became empowered?'[174]

But at the risk of disrespecting Lee's right to determine her own desires, one wonders how 'empowered' she really is. Her masochistic relationship with Edward sometimes seems to border on the non-consensual. Her love of pain could be problematic, especially since Edward's sadism doesn't always seem that different from her father's, and since her masochism is hard to separate from her self-harming. Does it matter that it is never she who spanks Edward? In playing the masochist, Lee may be as seriously stuck in the submissive 'female' role as she ever was.

VOYEURISM/EXHIBITIONISM

The Exterminating Angels
(Les anges exterminateurs) **(2006)**

Director: Jean-Claude Brisseau
Cast: Frédéric van den Driessche (François), Virginie Legeay (Virginie), Lise Bellynck (Julie), Maroussia Dubreuil (Charlotte)

Director Jean-Claude Brisseau was convicted of sexual harass-ment for having actresses masturbate in front of him as part of auditioning for his movie *Secret Things* (*Choses secrètes*) (2002). The charge was that he had used the prospect of film roles – which in the end they didn't get – to lure these women into exhibiting themselves for his own personal voyeuristic pleasure. During the trial, Brisseau came to believe that in reality he was being condemned by patriarchal society for revealing that women can find pleasure apart from men: 'When I said... in front of the judges that most girls like to caress themselves... that caused a scandal. I tell what I think is the truth, and because of that they instantly label me one of the perverts. They're total hypocrites!'[175]

Undaunted, Brisseau made *The Exterminating Angels* about a director (François) who auditions actresses by having them pleasure themselves in front of him. One actress, aptly named Virginie, who has never had an orgasm with her boyfriend ('he jumps me and, two minutes later, it's over'), finds that she is able to climax while masturbating for François, which she describes as a 'prohibited pleasure' that came 'like a revelation about my forbidden self'. What Virginie discovers is her own desire, facilitated by François who, because he is a 'stranger' and only watching, gives her the freedom to explore her own erotic fantasies. In another scene, François has actresses Julie and Charlotte touch each other under a table at a crowded restaurant, then later join another female performer for a threesome in a hotel bed. As Julie tells him, 'When I caressed myself in front of you, at first I hardly liked it, but then I suddenly felt an intense pleasure, which grew even stronger when I made love with Charlotte. It's because *you* were watching.' Julie can imagine François' male gaze as that of patriarchal disapproval, which only heightens her joy at breaking the taboo against female pleasure; and if one woman masturbating is taboo, how much more so is mutual masturbation or three women in a bed?

One could perhaps feel more confident that François/Brisseau was helping these women get in touch with their own desires and fantasies if he was not *directing* them from a position of visual and monetary power: after all, if their performance pleases *him*, he could cast them in his movie. Also, when he says he wants to 'convey the emotion of an encounter with mystical ecstasy as the actresses' pleasure ascends to orgasm', is this religio-sexual fantasy really theirs or his?

A Snake of June (Rokugatsu no hebi) (2002)

Director: Shinya Tsukamoto
Cast: Yuji Kotari (Shigehiko), Asuka Kurosawa (Rinko), Shinya Tsukamoto (Iguchi)

Because her husband Shigehiko neglects her, housewife Rinko turns to furtive masturbation. A mysterious caller (Iguchi) says that he will send photos of Rinko's shameful self-pleasuring to her husband unless she does what Iguchi orders. He has her go to a public mall and, knickerless and in a miniskirt, ride the escalator where she is exposed to onlookers below. The painfully shy Rinko is mortified, donning dark glasses and clutching an umbrella between her legs in a desperate attempt to cover up or at least remain anonymous. Next, Iguchi commands her to buy phallic-shaped vegetables, and he uses a remote control to activate the vibrator he has had her insert in her vagina, provoking shuddering orgasms which bring her to her knees and make her into a public spectacle. Although he seems to be blackmailing her into becoming an involuntary exhibitionist, Iguchi claims that he is merely pushing her beyond repression and inducing her to realise her own desires: 'I'm not trying to force you into sex. I just want you to do what you really want.' However, the fact that Rinko's sexual exposure is coerced rather than consensual, and that photographer Iguchi gets to watch her naked embarrassment without himself being seen, suggests that he is at least in part a sadistic voyeur.

Iguchi also coerces Shigehiko, inducing him to hallucinate that he is sitting with a group of men who, with funnels over their faces turning them into pinhole cameras, are compelled to watch a couple having sex and then drowning in a tank of water. In this way, Iguchi turns Shigehiko into a sadistic voyeur like himself, but he also brings the husband face-to-face with his greatest fear: that sex with his wife would overwhelm him with uncontrollable desire and orgasmic ecstasy. A neatness freak, Shigehiko is body-phobic and hygiene-obsessed, constantly cleaning the kitchen drain while afraid to use his own 'snake' on his wife. But, in another hallucination, Shigehiko is forced to watch a metallic phallus snake out from Iguchi's crotch and wrap around Shigehiko's neck, finally spraying him with black ooze. The husband must confront his fear of his own desire as dirty and mortifying.

In a rain-drenched scene, Shigehiko strokes the 'snake' in his pants while watching Rinko display her naked body and bring herself to orgasm with her own hands between her legs. The exhibitionism and voyeurism are now shared and voluntary, leading to a later scene where the husband and wife will both climax with him inside her, unafraid and unashamed to be flooded with desire.

Swimming Pool (2003)

Director: François Ozon
Cast: Charlotte Rampling (Sarah), Ludivine Sagnier (Julie), Jean-Marie Lamour (Franck)

Sarah is an 'old maid' author of British crime fiction who, suffering from writer's block, goes to a French country house for a freeing experience. There she spies on a young woman named Julie swimming naked in a pool and floating on her back, with her body arched to show off her breasts for the voyeur she knows is looking. Another time, Sarah sees Julie riding a man on a couch. Sarah is positioned so that the image of her watching face is reflected over the man's head as he throws it back in ecstasy, as though she were imagining herself in his place with Julie. In a further scene, a man named Franck fondles his own swim trunks while gazing down at Julie sunbathing and masturbating in a reclining chair, but a sudden cut takes us to Sarah moaning in her bedroom and then waking up, as if Franck's view of Julie had been Sarah's erotic dream. Earlier, she had told Julie that 'I'm going to be frank with you: I need peace and quiet to concentrate', but this statement turns out to have dissembled Sarah's true desire, which is to be *Franck* with Julie, to have her in the way that he does. Later, Sarah stands in Franck's same position above Julie, eyeing her bronzed and bikinied body stretched out beside the pool. Before taking a swim herself, Sarah finds a pair of Julie's panties near the pool and uses them for inspiration to write a new novel entitled *Julie*. One night Julie is dancing with Franck and invites Sarah to join them. (In the original script, this turned into a lesbian sex scene with him as the intermediary.) Then, after jealously watching Julie give Franck a blow job by the side of the pool, Sarah throws a rock into the water to get them to stop. Sarah later discovers that Julie smashed Franck's head in with a rock – in a sense only doing what Sarah wanted her to do, eliminating the man so that Sarah could have Julie all to herself. Sarah then seduces the gardener so that he won't find Franck's buried body. As the man caresses her, Sarah's eyes are closed for she is thinking in her excitement of Julie, who also has *her* eyes closed, thinking of Sarah. In this way, the voyeur and the exhibitionist – Sarah and Julie – are brought together through erotic fantasy. And it turns out that the whole thing, not only the crime but Julie herself, may have been a figment of Sarah's imagination, dreamed up as a plot for her latest fiction – though her desire was very real.

The Notorious Bettie Page (2005)

Director: Mary Harron
Cast: Gretchen Mol (Bettie)

As a girl, Bettie adopts fetching poses for a boy to take her picture with his homemade camera, then her father calls her into the house and molests her. A pattern is set: modelling becomes a way for Bettie to feel attractive to the male eye while also keeping her at a safe distance from the predations of men's lust. As long as she can keep them gazing, they're not groping; but, whenever there is physical contact beyond voyeurism, she finds herself exposed to violation. A seemingly nice young man invites Bettie to a dance but then takes her to a gang rape. Yet with another young man, a photographer, Bettie is willing to remove both her bikini top and bottoms, to exhibit herself completely nude. As director Mary Harron says, 'The distance between them is one reason why she feels safe, because he is behind the camera. ...It was the idea of a kind of reverse seduction: that if it was a very young, naïve photographer, she would enjoy taking control, and that she would be the one to say "I will take this off and that off", and she would enjoy the power of that.'[176] Bettie begins to wear spike-heeled boots and to wield a whip, pretending to lash other women as they model in sado-masochistic poses for a 'specialised' male clientele. In one bondage-and-discipline photo shoot, she lets her waist be cinched into a tight corset, her arms tied in a spread-eagle position and her mouth stuffed with a ball gag. Is Betty in control or is she conforming her body to sadistic male desires? Has their brutal gaze crossed over into sexual abuse, prompting her to model the pain they want her to suffer? Perhaps, but it is worth noting that Bettie preserves a sense of carefree innocence throughout these shoots, as if all the spankings and lashings were child's play. Like the girl who once posed for the boy next door, she seems to maintain the hope that, if she gives a pleasing enough performance, some nice young man will look on her with love and bridge that voyeuristic distance, finally bringing her physical fulfilment.

brilliantlove (The Orgasm Diaries) (2010)

Director: Ashley Horner
Cast: Liam Browne (Manchester), Nancy Trotter Landry (Noon)

Manchester and Noon are a young couple in love. When he first starts snapping nude and semi-nude photos of her, it is as a natural extension of their intimate relationship. He lifts her dress from behind to get a shot of her bottom. He takes pictures of her riding a bike naked. He even catches her squatting to urinate. Of course, director Ashley Horner is also filming the couple as they make love, and he tried to avoid 'echoing images that we see in pornography': 'Often I would use long, uninterrupted takes with simple camera movements and let the scene play right through, allowing you to follow the emotional journey of the characters rather than just thrusting you straight into the physical act of sex.'[177]

However, Manchester's own camerawork begins to blur 'the line between the erotic and the pornographic, between "art" and exploitation'.[178] In one scene, he thrusts vigorously into her and holds his hand over her mouth, taking photos as he comes. As a result, Noon bursts a blood vessel in her eye. Another time, after hours of being fucked and photographed from behind, she says she's 'too sore to carry on'. Yet, to oblige his desire, she recites a pornographic tale to him so that he can masturbate and ejaculate onto her backside. More and more, their sex is about *his* desire and she is pictured as fragmented body-parts for his onanistic satisfaction. 'My pussy's twice the size of my head,' she says about one photo. 'Is that how you see me?' She calls him 'a fucking dick' and a 'prick' to let him know what it feels like to be objectified, but he makes a deal to have his photos of her shown at an art gallery. Enraged at this unauthorised exhibition of herself, Noon leaves him.

Manchester gets drunk, drops his trousers and urinates before the eyes of the art show attendees, shaking his dick at them. By doing so, he expresses his contempt but he also renders himself exposed and vulnerable, as if punishing himself and putting himself in Noon's position to feel what she must have felt. (Throughout the film, Horner has shown as many shots of Manchester's penis as there are of Noon's vulva.) Missing her, Manchester tries to masturbate over a naked picture of Noon, but this pornographic substitute for her does not excite him. In despair – and to mete out the ultimate punishment for his selfish desire – he then tries to commit suicide by means of auto-erotic self-asphyxiation but is saved by Noon. In the end, the two of them are seen walking together through a field of green grass, reunited in love – and both fully clothed.

BIBLIOGRAPHY

Books

Andrews, David, *Soft in the Middle: The Contemporary Softcore Feature in Its Contexts*, Columbus: Ohio State University Press, 2006.

Anger, Kenneth, *Hollywood Babylon*, New York: Dell, 1975.

Atkins, Thomas R (ed), *Sexuality in the Movies*, New York: Da Capo Press, 1975.

Bell-Metereau, Rebecca, *Hollywood Androgyny*, New York: Columbia University Press, 1993.

Benshoff, Harry M, *Queer Images: A History of Gay and Lesbian Film in America*, Lanham: Rowman & Littlefield, 2005.

Benshoff, Harry M and Sean Griffin, *Queer Cinema: The Film Reader*, London: Routledge, 2004.

Bernard, Jami, *Total Exposure: The Movie Buff's Guide to Celebrity Nude Scenes*, Secaucus: Citadel Press, 1999.

Bernard, Jami (ed), *The X List: The National Society of Film Critics' Guide to the Movies That Turn Us On*, New York: Da Capo Press, 2005.

Bouzereau, Laurent, *The Cutting Room Floor*, Secaucus: Citadel Press, 1994.

Briggs, Joe Bob, *Profoundly Disturbing: Shocking Movies That Changed History!*, New York: Universe, 2003.

Briggs, Joe Bob, *Profoundly Erotic: Sexy Movies That Changed History*, New York: Universe, 2005.

Brode, Douglas, *Sinema: Erotic Adventures in Film*, Secaucus: Citadel Press, 2002.

Clover, Carol J, *Men, Women, and Chain Saws: Gender in the Modern Horror Film*, Princeton: Princeton University Press, 1992.

Davies, Steven Paul, *Out at the Movies: A History of Gay Cinema*, Harpenden: Kamera Books, 2008.

Dyer, Richard and Julianne Pidduck, *Now You See It: Studies on Lesbian and Gay Film*, London: Routledge, 2002.

Escoffier, Jeffrey, *Bigger than Life: The History of Gay Porn Cinema from Beefcake to Hardcore*, Philadelphia: Running Press, 2009.

Fentone, Steve, *AntiCristo: The Bible of Nasty Nun Sinema and Culture*, Godalming: FAB Press, 2000.

Flint, David, *Babylon Blue: An Illustrated History of Adult Cinema*, London: Creation Books, 1998.

Ford, Luke, *A History of X: 100 Years of Sex in Film*, Amherst: Prometheus Books, 1999.

Frank, Sam, *Sex in the Movies*, Secaucus: Citadel Press, 1986.

Fulwood, Neil, *One Hundred Sex Scenes That Changed Cinema*, London: Batsford, 2003.

Haskell, Molly, *From Reverence to Rape: The Treatment of Women in the Movies*, London: Penguin, 1974.

Hosoda, Craig, *The Bare Facts Video Guide: Where to Find Your Favorite Actors & Actresses Nude on Videotape*, Santa Clara: Bare Facts, 1995.

Hosoda, Craig, *The Bare Facts Video Guide: Where to Find Your Favorite Actresses Nude on Videotape*, Santa Clara: Bare Facts, 2001.

Hunter, Jack, *Eros in Hell: Sex, Blood and Madness in Japanese Cinema*, London: Creation Books, 1998.

Johnson, Bruce (ed), *Earogenous Zones: Sound, Sexuality and Cinema*. London: Equinox, 2010.

Kabir, Shameen, *Daughters of Desire: Lesbian Representations in Film*, London: Cassell, 1998.

Keesey, Douglas, *Erotic Cinema*, London: Taschen, 2005.

Keough, Peter (ed), *Flesh and Blood: The National Society of Film Critics on Sex, Violence, and Censorship*, San Francisco: Mercury House, 2005.

Krzywinska, Tanya, *Sex and the Cinema*, London: Wallflower Press, 2006.

Lang, Robert, *Masculine Interests: Homoerotics in Hollywood Film*, New York: Columbia University Press, 2002.

Lehman, Peter (ed), *Pornography: Film and Culture*, New Brunswick: Rutgers, 2006.

Lehman, Peter, *Running Scared: Masculinity and the Representation of the Male Body*, Detroit: Wayne State University Press, 2007.

Lehman, Peter and Susan Hunt, *Lady Chatterley's Legacy in the Movies: Sex, Brains, and Body Guys*, New Brunswick: Rutgers University Press, 2010.

Lenne, Gerard, *Sex on the Screen: Eroticism in Film*, New York: St Martin's Press, 1985.

Lenne, Gerard, *Sex on the Screen: The Eighties*, New York: St Martin's Press, 1990.

Lewis, Jon, *Hollywood v. Hard Core: How the Struggle Over Censorship Saved the Modern Film Industry*, New York: New York University Press, 2000.

Lort, Don, *Coming of Age: Movie and Video Guide*, Laguna Hills: Companion Press, 1997.

Loughlin, Gerard, *Alien Sex: The Body and Desire in Cinema and Theology*, Oxford: Blackwell, 2004.

Lyons, Charles, *The New Censors: Movies and the Culture Wars*, Philadelphia: Temple University Press, 1997.

Mainon, Dominique and James Ursini, *Cinema of Obsession: Erotic Fixation and Love Gone Wrong in the Movies*, New York: Limelight Editions, 2007.

Mainon, Dominique and James Ursini, *Femme Fatale: Cinema's Most Unforgettable Lethal Ladies*, New York: Limelight Editions, 2009.

Malone, Aubrey, *Censoring Hollywood: Sex and Violence in Film and on the Cutting Room Floor*, Jefferson: McFarland, 2011.

Martin, Nina K, *Sexy Thrills: Undressing the Erotic Thriller*, Urbana: University of Chicago Press, 2007.

Mathijs, Ernest and Xavier Mendik (eds), *Alternative Europe: Eurotrash and Exploitation Cinema Since 1945*, London: Wallflower Press, 2004.

McCarthy, Helen and Jonathan Clements, *The Erotic Anime Movie Guide*, Woodstock: Overlook Press, 1999.

McDonagh, Maitland, *The 50 Most Erotic Films of All Time*, Secaucus: Citadel Press, 1996.

Mr Skin, *Mr Skin's Skintastic Video Guide: The 501 Greatest Movies for Sex & Nudity on DVD*, Chicago: SK Books, 2007.

Muller, Eddie and Daniel Faris, *Grindhouse: The Forbidden World of 'Adults Only' Cinema*, New York: St Martin's Griffin, 1996.

Olson, Jenni, *The Queer Movie Poster Book*, San Francisco: Chronicle Books, 2004.

Pascall, Jeremy and Clyde Jeavons, *A Pictorial History of Sex in the Movies*, London: Hamlyn, 1975.

Paul, William, *Laughing Screaming: Modern Hollywood Horror and Comedy*, New York: Columbia University Press, 1994.

Pennington, Jody W, *The History of Sex in American Film*, London: Praeger, 2007.

Philips, Baxter, *Cut: The Unseen Cinema*, New York: Bounty Books, 1975.

Pollard, Tom, *Sex and Violence: The Hollywood Censorship Wars*, Boulder: Paradigm Publishers, 2010.

Radner, Hilary and Moya Luckett (eds), *Swinging Single: Representing Sexuality in the 1960s*, Minneapolis: University of Minnesota Press, 1999.

Rainer, Peter (ed), *Love and Hisses: The National Society of Film Critics Sound Off on the Hottest Movie Controversies*, San Francisco: Mercury House, 1992.

Rotsler, William, *Contemporary Erotic Cinema*, New York: Ballantine Books, 1973.

Russo, Vito, *The Celluloid Closet: Homosexuality in the Movies*, New York: Harper & Row, 1987.

Sharp, Jasper, *Behind the Pink Curtain: The Complete History of Japanese Sex Cinema*, Godalming: FAB Press, 2008.

Shipman, David, *Caught in the Act: Sex and Eroticism in the Movies*, London: Elm Tree Books, 1985.

Sinclair, Marianne, *Hollywood Lolitas: The Nymphet Syndrome in the Movies*, New York: Henry Holt, 1988.

Sova, Dawn B, *Forbidden Films: Censorship Histories of 125 Motion Pictures*, New York: Checkmark Books, 2001.

Springer, Claudia, *Electronic Eros: Bodies and Desire in the Postindustrial Age*, Austin: University of Texas Press, 1996.

Stevenson, Jack (ed), *Fleshpot: Cinema's Sexual Myth Makers & Taboo Breakers*, Manchester: Headpress, 2000.

Stevenson, Jack, *Scandinavian Blue: The Erotic Cinema of Sweden and Denmark in the 1960s and 1970s*, Jefferson: McFarland, 2010.

Stewart, Steve, *Full Frontal: Male Nudity Video Guide*, Laguna Hills: Companion Press, 1996.

Straayer, Chris, *Deviant Eyes, Deviant Bodies: Sexual Re-Orientation in Film and Video*, New York: Columbia University Press, 1996.

Tohill, Cathal and Pete Tombs, *Immoral Tales: European Sex and Horror Movies, 1956-1984*, New York: St Martin's Griffin, 1995.

Tropiano, Stephen, *Obscene, Indecent, Immoral, and Offensive: 100+ Years of Censored, Banned, and Controversial Films*, New York: Limelight Editions, 2009.

Tyler, Parker, *A Pictorial History of Sex in Films*, Secaucus: Citadel Press, 1974.

Tyler, Parker, *Screening the Sexes: Homosexuality in the Movies*, New York: Da Capo Press, 1993.

Weiss, Andrea, *Vampires & Violets: Lesbians in Film*, London: Penguin, 1993.

Williams, Linda, *Hard Core: Power, Pleasure, and the 'Frenzy of the Visible'*, Berkeley: University of California Press, 1999.

Williams, Linda (ed), *Porn Studies*, Durham: Duke University Press, 2004.

Williams, Linda, *Screening Sex*, Durham: Duke University Press, 2008.

Williams, Linda Ruth, *The Erotic Thriller in Contemporary Cinema*, Bloomington: Indiana University Press, 2005.

Wortley, Richard, *Erotic Movies*, London: Roxby Press, 1975.

160 Joe Orton, *The Orton Diaries*, ed. John Lahr, New York: Harper & Row, 1986, p. 106.

161 John Lahr, *Prick Up Your Ears: The Biography of Joe Orton*, New York: Knopf, 1978, p. 29.

162 Annabel Chong in Amy Goodman, 'An Interview with Annabel Chong', *Nerve*, 22 June 1999, http://www.nerve.com/dispatches/goodman/chong.

163 Ibid.

164 Annabel Chong in Gerrie Lim, *Singapore Rebel: Searching for Annabel Chong*, Singapore: Monsoon Books, 2011, p. 159.

165 Annabel Chong in Amy Goodman, 'An Interview with Annabel Chong', *Nerve*, 22 June 1999, http://www.nerve.com/dispatches/goodman/chong.

166 Annabel Chong in Robin Askew, 'Sex: The Annabel Chong Story', *Spike Magazine*, 1 October 2000, http://www.spikemagazine.com/1000annabelchong.php.

167 John Cameron Mitchell, 'How to Shoot Sex: A Docu-Primer', *Shortbus* DVD, TH!NKFilm, 2007.

168 John Cameron Mitchell in Mathew Hays, *The View from Here: Conversations with Gay and Lesbian Filmmakers*, Vancouver: Arsenal Pulp Press, 2007, pp. 221–2.

169 John Waters in David S Cohen, *Screen Plays*, New York: HarperCollins, 2008, p. 214.

170 John Waters interviewed on *This Film Is Not Yet Rated* DVD, Independent Film Channel, 2007.

171 John Waters in David S Cohen, *Screen Plays*, New York: HarperCollins, 2008, pp. 215–16.

172 Virginie Despentes, *Baise-moi*, trans. Bruce Benderson, New York: Grove Press, 2002, pp. 125–6.

173 Ibid., pp. 243–4.

174 Erin Cressida Wilson, *Secretary: A Screenplay*, Brooklyn: Soft Skull Press, 2003, pp. iv, vi.

175 Jean-Claude Brisseau, *L'ange exterminateur*, Paris: Grasset & Fasquelle, 2006, p. 199.

176 Mary Harron, Audiocommentary, *The Notorious Bettie Page* DVD, HBO, 2006.

177 Ashley Horner in 'Film Interview: *The Orgasm Diaries*', *Vegas Outsider*, http://vegas-outsider.com/articles/film/interviews/219-film-interview-the-orgasm-diaries-director-ashley-horner.

178 Ibid.